LET MY PEOPLE GO
A HAGGADAH

Illustrated by
MARK PODWAL

Introduction by
THEODORE BIKEL

DARIEN HOUSE, Inc.
New York City

THE FARMINGTON LIBRARY
FARMINGTON, CT 06032
DISCARD

296.19
LET

In memory of my uncle
David Appelbaum
Dubrova, Poland 1913 — Auschwitz, Poland 1944

©Copyright 1972, Darien House, Inc.
37 Riverside Drive, New York City 10023
All rights reserved.
Library of Congress Catalogue Card Number: 70-188878
ISBN 0-88201-002-6
Printed in the United States of America.

INTRODUCTION

Since the first printed Haggadah appeared in Guadalajara, Spain, some four hundred and ninety years ago this slim volume restricted in use to just two nights a year — one night if you reside in Israel — has probably become the most published of all Jewish books. At the turn of this century the bibliographer Samuel Wiener counted nine hundred and nine different editions of the Haggadah, noting that his list was most probably incomplete. This observation turned out to be accurate; later scholars and bibliographers uncovered many more editions and hundreds more have been added since. As of 1959 the library of the Jewish Theological Seminary in New York alone housed some two thousand different Haggadahs. Eleven years later the Israeli scholar Avraham Yaari listed two thousand seven hundred and thirteen editions of the Haggadah published in one hundred seventy different locations.

Thus, surely, it becomes appropriate for us to paraphrase the ancient question: 'How is this Haggadah different from all other Haggadahs?' And what purpose might be served by adding to the bookshelves yet another edition of a work whose supply most certainly exceeds all possible demand?

To my mind the answer to these questions is to be found in the Haggadah itself. A poignant passage of the Seder service, one which to many of us is central and fundamental to the commandment for the observance of Passover, states: "In every generation Man must look upon himself as if he personally had been freed from the bondage of Egypt." Thus the Passover ritual takes on an intensely personal and contemporary character. While remaining a holiday of Jewish national remembrance evoking, in fact, the very birth of Israel's peoplehood and celebrating the passage from oppression to independence it admonishes every Jew to seek the parallel in his own time and his own life to subjugation and redemption. Not only every Jew but every man is enjoined to continue the lesson of Passover and the cry of "Let My People Go" has been voiced by Jews and Gentiles alike whenever they were threatened by tyranny, enslavement, despotism and dictatorship.

There is indeed a constant updating within the Jewish consciousness, a drawing of parallels, a continuum of the group experience. For Pharaoh, read Titus or Torquemada, Chmielnicki, Czar Nicholas or Hitler, Stalin or Khrushchev or Kosygin. For the Jewish vision of deliverance from the yoke substitute no words — the feeling is self-regenerating and enduring.

The illustrations, of course, are what makes this Haggadah unique and extraordinary, timely and topical yet remaining fully within the context of the Jewish historical and emotional experience. Needless to say, the Haggadah itself is meant to be absolutely and strictly functional — fit for any Seder table.

Dr. Podwal's illustrations relate to the plight of the Jews in the Soviet Union as the contemporary version of Jews smarting under the whip of the oppressor. Whether the analogy appears apt to the casual and distant observer in the West is far less important than the feeling which emanates from every contact with Soviet Jews who have achieved their freedom and those still striving for it. To them the story of Passover is totally evocative of their own plight; even the underground poems and songs read and sung in cellars and basements in Moscow, Leningrad or Kiev draw heavily on the Passover theme. 'Pharaonu gavaryu, atpusti narod moi!' 'To you Pharaoh I say, let my people go!' 'Let the Hebrew people go to their proper homeland.' 'You hold us back at your own peril.' 'Let us go to the land where God alone has His domain, Let My People Go!'

Those are verses they sing. And at all times the focus is on Jerusalem; and Jerusalem means freedom from slavery.

If 'slavery' or the 'oppressor's whip' evoke an image of half-naked bodies being whipped by an overseer in a Siberian labor camp no such childish assumptions are in order. For in dealing with the phenomenon of anti-Semitism in any given place and time one must beware of facile descriptions and simplistic comparisons. While anti-Semitism everywhere and in any age has certain common characteristics the practice varies from time to time and from country to country. It encompasses all acts: from the barbarism of the auto-da-fé, the brutality of the pogrom and of its monstrous progeny, the Holocaust — to the more subtle and invidious harrassment of Jews by authorities, of quota systems for Jewish students, of vilification in the press; in short, everything from overt persecution to covert discrimination. One, cannot therefore, draw comparisons regarding the plight of the Jews during the Holocaust, for example, and the fate of their brothers under the Soviet regime. The Nazis were interested in one thing only: to destroy every last Jew physically, kill him, burn him, bury him. No such basic brutality seems to motivate those who control the fate of Jews in the Soviet Union. There the oppression centers not on the body but on the soul. Give up your Jewish soul and you shall live unharmed and unscathed. The catch is only that Jews have through centuries of persecution refused to part with the essence of their Jewishness; have even, when necessary, kept it alight and alive for generations in secret as they did following the Spanish Inquisition.

Still, while we are dealing here, by and large, not with physical extermination but with other forms of oppression it is well to remember that cultural genocide is also murder. And the anguish of a suffocating people is also martyrdom. Thus it seems entirely appropriate to speak of slavery in respect of the Jews in the USSR; for Jewish thought and Jewish teaching throughout the ages has always held exile and slavery to be synonymous.

> "This year we are here (in exile), next year in the land of Israel;
> this year we are slaves, next year free men."

So we chant at the beginning of the Seder. And again, at the end of the service: "Next year in Jerusalem." Jews of the Soviet Union many of whom are kept waiting for many agonizing months for an exit visa not only sing 'next year in Jersusalem' with fervor but their impatience and frustration moves them to alter the ancient words to hasten deliverance: 'This year in Jerusalem.'

The issue of Soviet Jewry has provoked many reactions in the world. They range from the irrational, boorish and violent — and therefore unproductive — to the soft-pedaling and velvet-glove approach — equally unproductive. To my mind the true course lies in positive, forceful, non-violent and constant action, never ceasing to remind the world and the Soviet leadership of the mark of shame on the Soviet conscience. If there is moral pressure to be applied then the means employed must be moral ones also. The plight of the Soviet Jews must be dealt with directly and in an unencumbered fashion; it is not a vehicle for other issues or polemics. For example, those who look to Soviet Jewry to be used as yet another stick in general anti-Communist crusades should go elsewhere in their quest. For the objective of all responsible action in this area is not to oppose Soviet foreign policies or gather debating points in East-West confrontations but solely to support the aspirations of Soviet Jewry in their quest for freedom.

If there are those who would take it into their own hands to visit ten plagues upon the Soviet oppressor, they might be reminded that this is God's prerogative not man's. Even when the angels rejoiced at the ultimate downfall of the enemy the Lord sternly rebuked them: 'The fruit of my handiwork is drowning in the sea and you dare to sing praises?' Perhaps also we should ponder the significance of our custom of removing ten drops of wine from our cup while reciting the plagues. This we do to remind ourselves that death or suffering — even of a deadly enemy — means the loss of a drop of joy from the cup of life.

Passover represents not only remembrance of deep scars and memories of past persecution. It is no coincidence that Passover is to be celebrated in the spring; for it also is meant to carry a message of hope and anticipation. The rays of the spring sun and the fresh blossoms herald new beginnings and offer hope for harvests to come. Mark Podwal's illustrations which accompany the ancient text of this Haggadah remind us of fresh wounds; yet the faith in Israel's indomitable spirit is also Passover. Justice will prevail and our brethren will be saved through our efforts and with considerable help from above. Hopefully, in years to come this Haggadah will be in use in Jewish homes with children seeing in these pictures only another chapter in the long Jewish history of suffering and deprivation — but a chapter of the past.

— THEODORE BIKEL.

August 6, 1969

To the Commission on Human Rights
United Nations
New York, USA

We 18 religious Jewish families of Georgia request you to help us leave for Israel. Each one of us, upon receiving an invitation from a relative in Israel, obtained the necessary questionnaires from the authorized USSR agencies and filled them out. Each was assured orally that no obstacles would be put in the way of his departure. Expecting to receive permission any day, each sold his property and gave up his job. But long months have gone by — years, for many — and permission for departure has not yet been given. We have sent hundreds of letters and telegrams; they have vanished like tears in the sand of the desert. All we hear are one-syllable oral refusals. We see no written replies. No one explains anything. No one cares about our fate.

But we are waiting, for we believe in God.

We 18 religious Jewish families of Georgia consider it necessary to explain why we want to go to Israel.

Everybody knows how just national policy, the theoretical principals of which were formulated long ago by the founder of the state, V. I. Lenin, is in fact being carried out in the USSR. There have not been pogroms, pales, and quotas in the country for a long, long time. Jews can walk the streets without fear for their lives; they can live where they wish, hold any position, even as high as the post of minister, is is evident from the example of V. Dymshits, Deputy Chairman of the USSR Council of Ministers. There is even a Jewish deputy in the Supreme Soviet — A. Chakovsky, Editor-in-Chief of Literaturnaya Gazeta.

Therefore, it is not racial discrimination that compels us to leave the country. Then perhaps it is religious discrimination? But synagogues are permitted in the country, and we are not prohibited from praying at home. However, our prayers are with Israel, for it is written: "If I forget thee, O Jerusalem, may my right hand forget its cunning." For we religious Jews feel that there is no Jew without faith, just as there is no faith without traditions. What, then, is our faith and what are our traditions?

For a long time the Roman legions besieged Jerusalem. But despite the well-known horrors of the siege — hunger, lack of water, disease, and much more — the Jews did not renounce their faith and did not surrender. However, man's strength has its limits, too, and in the end barbarians broke into the Holy City. Thus, 1,900 years ago, the Holy Temple was destroyed, and with it the Jewish State. The nation, however, remained. Although the Jews who could bear arms did not surrender to the enemy and killed one another, there remained the old people, women and children.

And whoever could not get away was killed on the spot.

But whoever could went away into the desert; and whoever survived reached other countries — to believe, to pray, to wait.

Henceforth they had to find a way to live in alien lands among people who hated them. Showered with insults, covered with the mud of slander, despised and persecuted, they earned their daily bread with blood and sweat, and reared their children.

Their hands were calloused, their souls were drenched in blood. But the important thing is that the nation was not destroyed — and what a nation!

The Jews gave the world religion and revolutionaries, philosophers and scholars, wealthy men and wise men, geniuses with the hearts of children, and children with the eyes of old people. There is no field of knowledge, no branch of literature and art to which Jews have not contributed their share. There is no country which gave Jews shelter which has not been repaid by their labor. And what did the Jews get in return?

When life was bearable for all, the Jews waited fearfully for other times. And when life became bad for all, the Jews knew that their last hour had come, and then they hid or ran away from the country.

And whoever got away began from the beginning again.

And whoever could not run away was destroyed.

And whoever hid well waited until other times came.

Who did not persecute the Jews? Everybody joined in baiting them.

When untalented generals lost a war, those to blame for the defeat were found at once — Jews. When a political adventurer did not keep the mountain of promises he had given, a reason was found at once — the Jews. Jews died in the torture chambers of the Inquisition in Spain and in Fascist concentration camps in Germany. Anti-Semites raised a scare — in enlightened France it was the Dreyfus case; in illiterate Russia, the Beilis case.

And the Jews had to endure everything.

But there was a way that they could have lived tranquilly, like other peoples; all they had to do was convert to another faith. Some did this — there are cowards everywhere. But millions preferred a life of suffering and often death to apostasy.

And even if they did wander the earth without shelter, God found a place for all.

And even if their ashes are scattered through the world, the memory of them is alive.

Their blood is in our veins, and our tears are their tears.

The prophecy has come true: Israel has risen from the ashes; we have not forgotten Jerusalem, and it needs our hands.

There are 18 of us who signed this letter. But he errs who thinks there are only 18 of us. There could could have been many more signatures.

They say there is a total of 12,000,000 Jews in the world. But he errs who believes there is a total of 12,000,000 of us. For with those who pray for Israel are hundreds of millions who did not live to this day, who were tortured to death, who are no longer here. They march shoulder to shoulder with us, unconquered and immortal, those who handed down to us the traditions of struggle and faith.

That is why we want to go Israel.

History has entrusted the United Nations with a great mission — to think about people and help them. Therefore, we demand that the United Nations Human Rights Commission do everything it can to obtain from the Soviet Government in the shortest possible time permission for us to leave. It is incomprehensive that in the 20th century people can be prohibited from living where they wish to live. It is strange that it is possible to forget the widely publicized appeals about the right of nations to self-determination — and, of course, the right of the people who comprise the nation.

We will wait months and years, we will wait all our lives if necessary, but we will not renounce our faith or our hopes.

We believe: our prayers have reached God.

We know: our appeals will reach people.

For we are asking — let us go to the land of our forefathers.

NOTES ON THIS HAGGADAH

Last year I came across the letter sent by the eighteen Jewish families of the Soviet Union to the Commission on Human Rights (reproduced on the preceding pages) which argues so eloquently for the right of Soviet Jews to emigrate to the land of their forefathers. As a Jew, I was extremely moved by the words; as an artist, I felt an overwhelming urge to somehow illustrate this letter. After completing several drawings I became dissatisfied with my efforts and set the work aside. But at the Seder during the last Passover, I realized that there was only one effective way to illustrate this moving letter: to create an entire Haggadah based on the plight of Soviet Jews.

After carefully studying the text of the Haggadah and reading over one hundred examples of this well-known story of the Jewish exodus and deliverance, of bondage and freedom, it became quite apparent to me that the words of the Haggadah are as relevant today as when they were first set down. The actual drawings seen here were created between October and December 1971.

Recent Jewish history has influenced modern Haggadah illustration. Several versions are concerned with the theme of the horrors perpetrated by the Nazis. A rather unique document is a booklet which was created in 1937 by several German-Jewish boys who had been rescued from concentration camps. Although, as Theodore Bikel aptly points out, we cannot compare the intentions of the Nazis with those of the Soviet Union, the ancient words of the Haggadah — "In every generation men rise up against us" — are nevertheless pertinent to the situation Soviet Jews find themselves in today.

For all these reasons I have made the illustrations as relevant as the text. The land of Egypt becomes the Soviet Union, and Pharaoh suddenly bears striking resemblance to the Czar Nicholas II. In addition, I have tried to incorporate into my drawings some of the mystery associated with the miracles and wonders of the feast of Passover. The plagues spring forth from those objects in our daily lives which symbolize the existence of our God. Flies come forth from tephillin boxes as hail is blown forth from the shofar.

The text for this Haggadah is taken from *The Standard Haggadah* published by Bloch Publishing Company, Inc., New York City. I am most grateful to Mr. Charles E. Bloch for permission to use this text and for his kind interest in this project. In some instances, I have changed the translation slightly to make the language a little more clear and direct. Also, I have added "The Matzoh of Hope" (page 16), a special Passover prayer which the American Jewish Conference on Soviet Jewry suggests be read at the Seder of every American Jewish household. I strongly concur. The preceding letter of the Soviet Jews is the full text, less signatures, as it appears in the excellent book, *Let My People Go*, edited by Richard Cohen (Popular Library: New York City, 1971).

Many individuals lent their assistance to this volume; I am grateful to all of them, and can only mention a few names here:

Theodore Bikel has done more than write an introduction. His wholehearted involvement in this book and his warm personal encouragement and insightful suggestions were those not only of a warm human being but a concerned scholar as well.

Julius Schatz, the Director of the Commission on Jewish Affairs of the American Jewish Congress, has been of invaluable assistance and great encouragement. Aida Dornbrand has given me much good advice regarding the artistic merits of the drawings. I also received a good deal of encouragement from Stanley and Arlene Katz, Dr. and Mrs. Lawrence Frank, Dr. Y. Rapp, as well as my parents and brother, Milton, Dorothy and David Podwal. Rabbi Yaakov Jacobs looked over my shoulder before this Haggadah went to press; I thank him for his advice.

Because time was very short, and so many advised me that it could not be published in time, I am especially appreciative of those individuals whose work on the physical production and distribution of this book, ignoring the impossible, made possible its timely and attractive appearance. Jack Rennert, my publisher, said "Let's do it!" after seeing only a few sketches two months before going to press. Harry Chester, who did all the design and production work on the book under much pressure of time, is especially to be thanked: It is a far better book for his contribution. Andrew Merson, who printed this book in record time, showed much more concern and interest than one has a right to expect of a printer. Clerical help, with a smile and efficiency, came from Vivian Rowan and Valerie Beale.

Almost 60 years have passed since Mendel Beleis was falsely accused and tried for allegedly murdering a Christian boy and using his blood for the baking of Passover matzohs, in Kiev, Russia. Today, Jews continue to stand trial in the Soviet Union. However, this time the Jews are actually guilty of what they are accused: the desire to live as Jews, whether in their adopted country or in the land of their forefathers.

—Mark Podwal, January 1972.

ORDER OF SERVICE

KADDESH:
Recite the *Kiddush,* or Sanctification of the Festival.

U'RHATZ:
Wash the hands without pronouncing the benediction.

KARPAS:
Partake of parsley dipped in salt water.

YAHATZ:
Divide the middle matzah, and hide the bigger part to be eaten at the end of the meal as the *aphikoman.*

MAGGID:
Recite the *Haggadah.*

RAHATZ:
Wash the hands pronoucing the prescribed benediction.

MOTZI; MATZAH:
Pronouce the benedictions *Hamotzi and Matzah.*

MAROR:
Eat the bitter herbs.

KOREKH:
Combine matzah and horseradish and eat them together.

SHULHAN OREKH:
Partake of the festival meal.

TZAFOON:
Eat the aphikoman.

BOREKH:
Recite the grace after meals.

HALLEL:
Recite the Hallel Psalms.

NIRTZAH:
Praying for the divine acceptance of our service.

KADDESH:

Sanctification of the Passover
On Friday evening begin here:

And it was evening and it was morning, the sixth day. The heavens and the earth, and their hosts were finished.
On the seventh day God finished the work which He had done; and He rested on the seventh day from all His work which He had done. God blessed the seventh day and hallowed it; for the reason that in it He rested from all His work of the creation.

On week days begin here:

Blessed art Thou, O Lord our God, King of the universe, Creator of the fruit of the vine.

On Friday evening, add the words in the brackets

Blessed art Thou, O Lord our God, King of the universe, for having chosen us from all peoples, for having exalted us above all nations, and for having sanctified us with Thy commandments. In love, hast Thou, O Lord our God, given us [Sabbaths for rest, and] solemn days of joy and festive seasons of gladness, even [this Sabbath, and] this Feast of Unleavened Bread, the season of our liberation, a holy convocation [in love] to commemorate the departure from Egypt. Thou hast chosen us and sanctified us above all peoples, and Thou hast made us share [in the blessing of] the [Sabbath, and of] the holy festivals, to be observed [with love and favor] in happiness and gladness. Blessed art Thou, O Lord, who hast sanctified [the Sabbath, and] Israel and the festive seasons.

On Saturday night add the following paragraphs:

Blessed art Thou, O Lord our God, King of the universe, Creator of the light of the fire.
Blessed art Thou, O Lord our God, King of the universe, who hast distinguished between the sacred and the profane, between light and darkness, between Israel and other nations, between the seventh day and the six working days. Thou hast distinguished between the holiness of the Sabbath and the holiness of the feast-days, and Thou hast hallowed the seventh day above the six working days. Thou hast distinguished Thy people Israel, and Thou hast hallowed them with Thy holiness. Blessed art Thou, O Lord our God, who hast distinguished between two kinds of holiness.

(וַיְהִי עֶרֶב וַיְהִי בֹקֶר

יוֹם הַשִּׁשִּׁי. וַיְכֻלּוּ הַשָּׁמַיִם וְהָאָרֶץ וְכָל צְבָאָם. וַיְכַל אֱלֹהִים בַּיּוֹם הַשְּׁבִיעִי מְלַאכְתּוֹ אֲשֶׁר עָשָׂה, וַיִּשְׁבֹּת בַּיּוֹם הַשְּׁבִיעִי מִכָּל מְלַאכְתּוֹ אֲשֶׁר עָשָׂה. וַיְבָרֶךְ אֱלֹהִים אֶת יוֹם הַשְּׁבִיעִי וַיְקַדֵּשׁ אֹתוֹ, כִּי בוֹ שָׁבַת מִכָּל מְלַאכְתּוֹ אֲשֶׁר בָּרָא אֱלֹהִים לַעֲשׂוֹת.)

סָבְרֵי מָרָנָן וְרַבּוֹתַי.

בָּרוּךְ אַתָּה, יְיָ אֱלֹהֵינוּ, מֶלֶךְ הָעוֹלָם, בּוֹרֵא פְּרִי הַגָּפֶן.

בָּרוּךְ אַתָּה, יְיָ אֱלֹהֵינוּ, מֶלֶךְ הָעוֹלָם, אֲשֶׁר בָּחַר בָּנוּ מִכָּל עָם, וְרוֹמְמָנוּ מִכָּל לָשׁוֹן, וְקִדְּשָׁנוּ בְּמִצְוֹתָיו. וַתִּתֶּן־לָנוּ, יְיָ אֱלֹהֵינוּ, בְּאַהֲבָה (שַׁבָּתוֹת לִמְנוּחָה וּ)מוֹעֲדִים לְשִׂמְחָה, חַגִּים וּזְמַנִּים לְשָׂשׂוֹן, אֶת יוֹם (הַשַּׁבָּת הַזֶּה, וְאֶת יוֹם) חַג הַמַּצּוֹת הַזֶּה, זְמַן חֵרוּתֵנוּ, (בְּאַהֲבָה) מִקְרָא קֹדֶשׁ, זֵכֶר לִיצִיאַת מִצְרָיִם. כִּי בָנוּ בָחַרְתָּ, וְאוֹתָנוּ קִדַּשְׁתָּ מִכָּל הָעַמִּים, (וְשַׁבָּת) וּמוֹעֲדֵי קָדְשֶׁךָ (בְּאַהֲבָה וּבְרָצוֹן) בְּשִׂמְחָה וּבְשָׂשׂוֹן הִנְחַלְתָּנוּ. בָּרוּךְ אַתָּה, יְיָ, מְקַדֵּשׁ (הַשַּׁבָּת וְ)יִשְׂרָאֵל וְהַזְּמַנִּים.

(בָּרוּךְ אַתָּה, יְיָ אֱלֹהֵינוּ, מֶלֶךְ הָעוֹלָם, בּוֹרֵא מְאוֹרֵי הָאֵשׁ.

בָּרוּךְ אַתָּה, יְיָ אֱלֹהֵינוּ, מֶלֶךְ הָעוֹלָם, הַמַּבְדִּיל בֵּין קֹדֶשׁ לְחֹל, בֵּין אוֹר לְחֹשֶׁךְ, בֵּין יִשְׂרָאֵל לָעַמִּים, בֵּין יוֹם הַשְּׁבִיעִי לְשֵׁשֶׁת יְמֵי הַמַּעֲשֶׂה. בֵּין קְדֻשַּׁת שַׁבָּת לִקְדֻשַּׁת יוֹם טוֹב הִבְדַּלְתָּ, וְאֶת יוֹם הַשְּׁבִיעִי מִשֵּׁשֶׁת יְמֵי הַמַּעֲשֶׂה קִדַּשְׁתָּ; הִבְדַּלְתָּ וְקִדַּשְׁתָּ אֶת עַמְּךָ יִשְׂרָאֵל בִּקְדֻשָּׁתֶךָ. בָּרוּךְ אַתָּה, יְיָ, הַמַּבְדִּיל בֵּין קֹדֶשׁ לְקֹדֶשׁ.)

Blessed art Thou, O Lord our God, King of the universe, who hast kept us alive and hast sustained us to reach this festive season.

בָּרוּךְ אַתָּה, יְיָ אֱלֹהֵינוּ, מֶלֶךְ הָעוֹלָם, שֶׁהֶחֱיָנוּ וְקִיְּמָנוּ
וְהִגִּיעָנוּ לַזְּמַן הַזֶּה.

Drink the first cup of wine.

ברוך אתה יי אלהינו מלך העולם
שהחינו וקימנו והגיענו לזמן הזה:

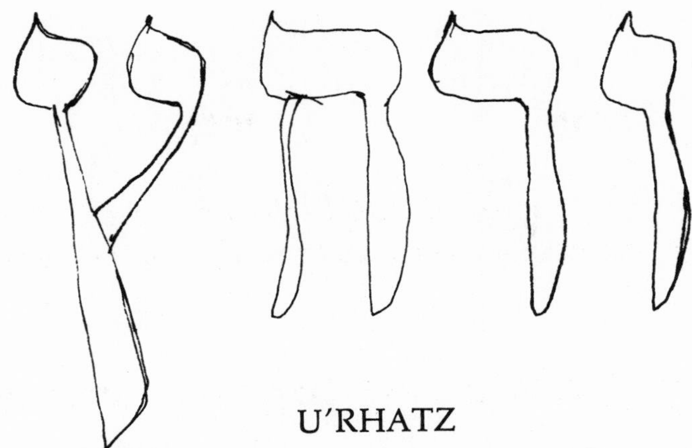

U'RHATZ

Wash the hands without pronouncing the benediction.

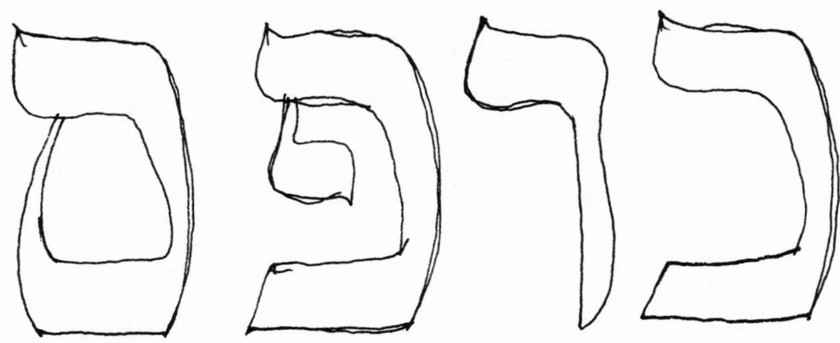

KARPAS

Dip parsley or lettuce in salt water or in vinegar, and recite the following benediction:

Blessed art Thou, O Lord our God, King of the universe, Creator of the fruit of the earth.

בָּרוּךְ אַתָּה, יְיָ אֱלֹהֵינוּ, מֶלֶךְ הָעוֹלָם, בּוֹרֵא פְּרִי הָאֲדָמָה.

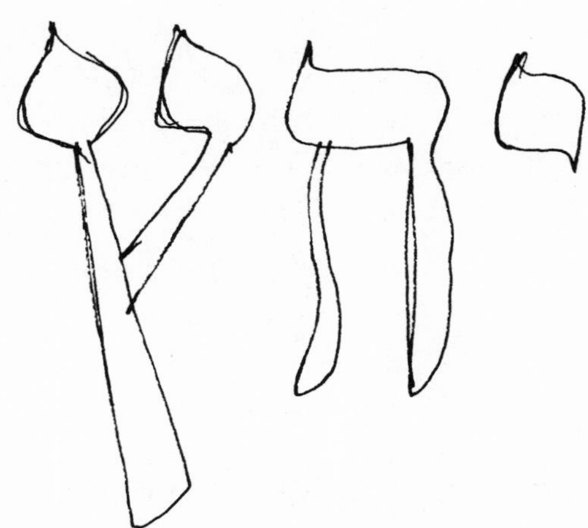

YAHATZ:

The leader breaks the middle matzah, leaves one-half in its place, and hides the other half to be eaten as the aphikoman at the end of the meal.

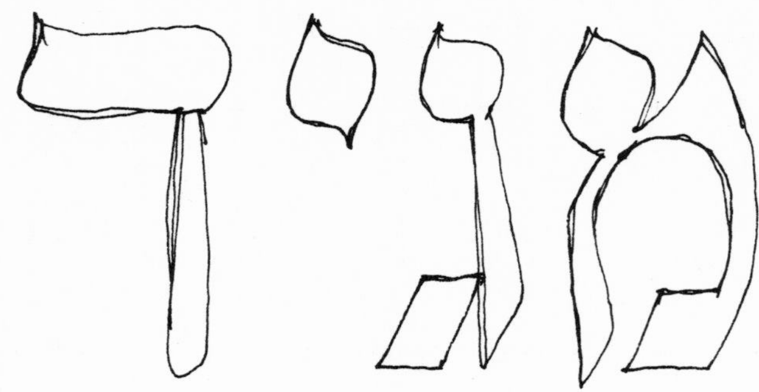

MAGGID

Now the Haggadah is recited; the leader raises the matzoth and says:

Lo! this is the bread of affliction which our fathers ate in the land of Egypt. Let all who are hungry come and eat. Let all who are in want come and celebrate the Passover with us. This year we are here, next year we shall be in the land of Israel. This year we are in servitude, next year we shall be free men.

הָא לַחְמָא עַנְיָא דִּי אֲכָלוּ אַבְהָתָנָא בְּאַרְעָא דְמִצְרָיִם.
כָּל דִּכְפִין יֵיתֵי וְיֵיכֻל, כָּל דִּצְרִיךְ יֵיתֵי וְיִפְסַח.
הָשַׁתָּא הָכָא, לַשָּׁנָה הַבָּאָה בְּאַרְעָא דְיִשְׂרָאֵל.
הָשַׁתָּא עַבְדֵי, לַשָּׁנָה הַבָּאָה בְּנֵי חוֹרִין.

This is the matzah of hope

This matzah, which we set aside as a symbol of hope for the three and a half million Jews of the Soviet Union, reminds us of the indestructible links that exist between us.

As we observe this festival of freedom, we know that Soviet Jews are not free — not free to leave, not free to learn of their Jewish past or to hand it down to their children. They cannot learn the languages of their fathers. They cannot teach their children to be the teachers, and the rabbis of future generations.

As they courageously assert their proud determination to live in Israel, we add our voices to theirs, and we shall be joined by all whose consciences are aroused by the wrongs inflicted on Soviet Jews. Thus shall they know that they have not been forgotten and they shall yet emerge into the light of freedom.

In 1962 the baking of matzoth for Passover was prohibited in the Soviet Union. After Jews from all over the free world raised their voices in protest, the ban was relaxed somewhat for the Jews of Moscow. Finally, in 1969, the baking of matzoth was permitted for Jews throughout the Soviet Union.

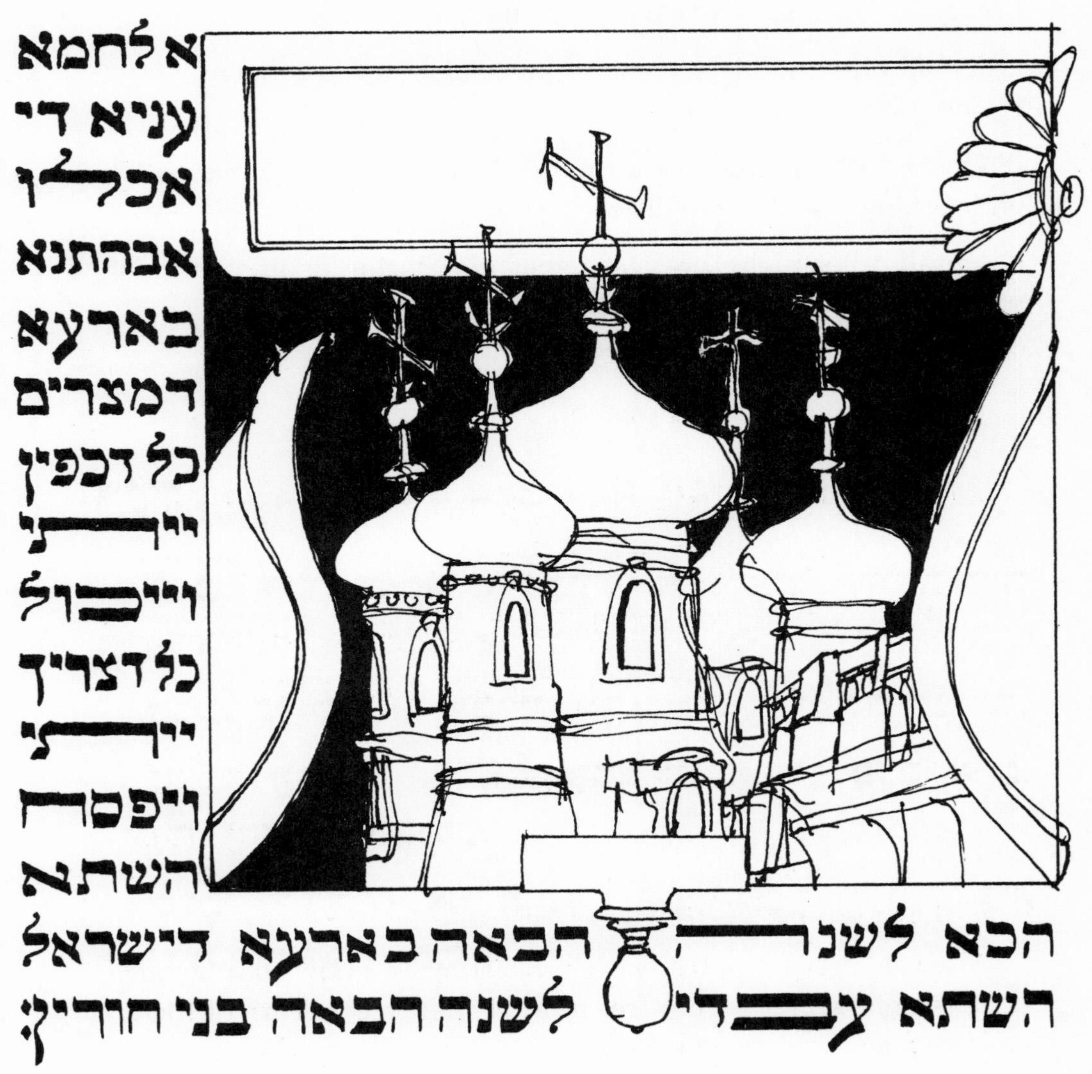

א לחמא
עניא די
אכלו
אבהתנא
בארעא
דמצרים
כל דכפין
ייתי
וייכול
כל דצריך
ייתי
ויפסח
השתא
הכא לשנה הבאה בארעא דישראל
השתא עבדי לשנה הבאה בני חורין:

The second cup is filled, and the youngest person at the table asks:

Why is this night different from all other nights?

On all other nights, we may eat either leavened or unleavened bread; on this night, we eat only unleavened bread.

On all other nights, we eat all kinds of herbs; on this night, we eat only bitter herbs.

On all other nights, we do not dip (the vegetables) even once; on this night, we have to dip them twice.

On all other nights, we eat either in a sitting or in a reclining position; on this night, we all recline.

מַה נִּשְׁתַּנָּה הַלַּיְלָה הַזֶּה מִכָּל הַלֵּילוֹת.

שֶׁבְּכָל הַלֵּילוֹת אָנוּ אוֹכְלִין חָמֵץ וּמַצָּה, הַלַּיְלָה הַזֶּה כֻּלּוֹ מַצָּה.

שֶׁבְּכָל הַלֵּילוֹת אָנוּ אוֹכְלִין שְׁאָר יְרָקוֹת, הַלַּיְלָה הַזֶּה מָרוֹר.

שֶׁבְּכָל הַלֵּילוֹת אֵין אָנוּ מַטְבִּילִין אֲפִילוּ פַּעַם אֶחָת, הַלַּיְלָה הַזֶּה שְׁתֵּי פְעָמִים.

שֶׁבְּכָל הַלֵּילוֹת אָנוּ אוֹכְלִין בֵּין יוֹשְׁבִין וּבֵין מְסֻבִּין, הַלַּיְלָה הַזֶּה כֻּלָּנוּ מְסֻבִּין.

מה נשתנה הלילה הזה
מכל הלילות?
שבכל הלילות אנו אוכלין
חמץ ומצה; הלילה הזה
כלו מצה.
שבכל הלילות אנו אוכלין
שאר ירקות: הלילה הזה
מרור.
שבכל הלילות אין אנו מטבילין
אפילו פעם אחת; הלילה
הזה שתי פעמים.
שבכל הלילות אנו אוכלין
בין יושבין ובין מסבין; הלילה
הזה כלנו מסבין.

The leader and the group then answer:

We were Pharaoh's slaves in Egypt.
But the Lord our God brought us out of there with a mighty hand and an outstretched arm. Had not the Holy One, blessed be He, brought forth our fathers from Egypt, we, our children, and our children's children would have remained Pharaoh's slaves in Egypt. Therefore, even if all of us were wise, men of understanding, sages, and well versed in the Torah, it would still be our duty to tell the story of the deliverance from Egypt. And the more one tells of the deliverance from Egypt, the more praiseworthy he is.

עֲבָדִים הָיִינוּ לְפַרְעֹה בְּמִצְרָיִם, וַיּוֹצִיאֵנוּ יְיָ אֱלֹהֵינוּ מִשָּׁם
בְּיָד חֲזָקָה וּבִזְרוֹעַ נְטוּיָה. וְאִלּוּ לֹא הוֹצִיא הַקָּדוֹשׁ בָּרוּךְ הוּא
אֶת אֲבוֹתֵינוּ מִמִּצְרָיִם, הֲרֵי אָנוּ וּבָנֵינוּ, וּבְנֵי בָנֵינוּ, מְשֻׁעְבָּדִים
הָיִינוּ לְפַרְעֹה בְּמִצְרָיִם. וַאֲפִילוּ כֻּלָּנוּ חֲכָמִים, כֻּלָּנוּ נְבוֹנִים,
כֻּלָּנוּ זְקֵנִים, כֻּלָּנוּ יוֹדְעִים אֶת הַתּוֹרָה, מִצְוָה עָלֵינוּ לְסַפֵּר
בִּיצִיאַת מִצְרָיִם. וְכָל הַמַּרְבֶּה לְסַפֵּר בִּיצִיאַת מִצְרָיִם הֲרֵי
זֶה מְשֻׁבָּח.

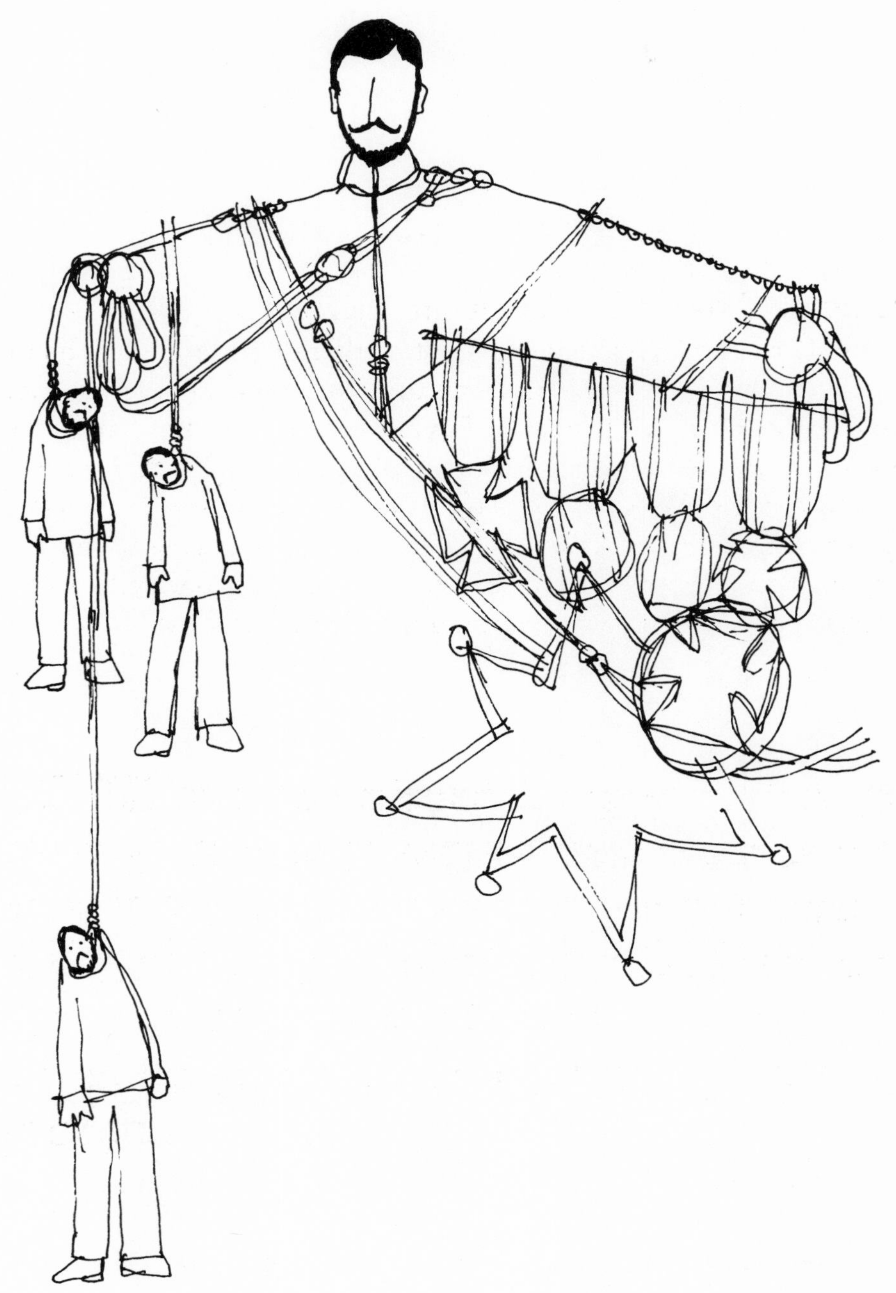

It is told of Rabbi Eliezer, Rabbi Joshua, Rabbi Eleazar ben Azariah, Rabbi Akiba and Rabbi Tarfon, that they once celebrated the Passover in B'ne B'rak, and that they spent the whole night in telling the story of the departure from Egypt, till their disciples came and said: "Our masters, the time has arrived for the reading of the morning prayers!"

Said Rabbi Eleazer ben Azariah: "I am about seventy years old, and I have not succeeded in proving that the story of the deliverance from Egypt should be told at night, until Ben Zoma explained it thus: 'It is written: That you may remember the day of your departure from Egypt all the days of your life. *Days* of your life would signify *days* only, but all the days of your life includes the nights as well.' The sages, however, differ and explain it thus: '*Days* of your life would have reference to our present life, while *all* the days of your life includes also the Messianic era.' "

מַעֲשֶׂה בְּרַבִּי אֱלִיעֶזֶר וְרַבִּי יְהוֹשֻׁעַ, וְרַבִּי אֶלְעָזָר בֶּן עֲזַרְיָה וְרַבִּי עֲקִיבָא וְרַבִּי טַרְפוֹן, שֶׁהָיוּ מְסֻבִּין בִּבְנֵי בְרַק, וְהָיוּ מְסַפְּרִים בִּיצִיאַת מִצְרַיִם כָּל אוֹתוֹ הַלַּיְלָה, עַד שֶׁבָּאוּ תַלְמִידֵיהֶם וְאָמְרוּ לָהֶם: רַבּוֹתֵינוּ, הִגִּיעַ זְמַן קְרִיאַת שְׁמַע שֶׁל שַׁחֲרִית.

אָמַר רַבִּי אֶלְעָזָר בֶּן עֲזַרְיָה: הֲרֵי אֲנִי כְּבֶן שִׁבְעִים שָׁנָה, וְלֹא זָכִיתִי שֶׁתֵּאָמֵר יְצִיאַת מִצְרַיִם בַּלֵּילוֹת עַד שֶׁדְּרָשָׁהּ בֶּן זוֹמָא, שֶׁנֶּאֱמַר: לְמַעַן תִּזְכֹּר אֶת יוֹם צֵאתְךָ מֵאֶרֶץ מִצְרַיִם כֹּל יְמֵי חַיֶּיךָ. יְמֵי חַיֶּיךָ הַיָּמִים; כֹּל יְמֵי חַיֶּיךָ הַלֵּילוֹת. וַחֲכָמִים אוֹמְרִים: יְמֵי חַיֶּיךָ הָעוֹלָם הַזֶּה; כֹּל יְמֵי חַיֶּיךָ לְהָבִיא לִימוֹת הַמָּשִׁיחַ.

Blessed be the Eternal; blessed be He! Blessed be He who has given the Torah to His people Israel; blessed be He!

The Torah (in explaining the meaning of the Passover) speaks of four types of sons: the wise, the wicked, the simple, and the one who is unable to inquire.

בָּרוּךְ הַמָּקוֹם, בָּרוּךְ הוּא. בָּרוּךְ שֶׁנָּתַן תּוֹרָה לְעַמּוֹ יִשְׂרָאֵל, בָּרוּךְ הוּא.

כְּנֶגֶד אַרְבָּעָה בָנִים דִּבְּרָה תוֹרָה: אֶחָד חָכָם, וְאֶחָד רָשָׁע, וְאֶחָד תָּם, וְאֶחָד שֶׁאֵינוֹ יוֹדֵעַ לִשְׁאוֹל.

What does the wise son ask? "What is the meaning of the testimonies, the statutes and the ordinances which the Lord our God has commanded you?"

To him you must explain all the laws concerning the Passover, even the law that no dessert may be eaten after the eating of the paschal lamb.

What does the wicked son ask? "What mean you by this service?" By saying *you*, he excludes himself from the community, thereby denying a fundamental principle (in Judaism). Therefore you shall reply: "It is because of that which the Lord did for *me* when *I* came out of Egypt"; for me but not for him, for had he been there, he would not have been redeemed.

What does the simple son ask? "What is this?" To him you shall say: "By strength of hand the Lord brought us out of Egypt, out of the house of bondage."

As for the son who is unable to inquire, you must broach the subject to him, as it is said: "You shall tell your son on that day, saying: 'It is because of that which the Lord did for me when I came out of Egypt.' "

חָכָם מַה הוּא אוֹמֵר: מָה הָעֵדֹת וְהַחֻקִּים וְהַמִּשְׁפָּטִים אֲשֶׁר צִוָּה יְיָ אֱלֹהֵינוּ אֶתְכֶם. וְאַף אַתָּה אֱמָר־לוֹ כְּהִלְכוֹת הַפֶּסַח, אֵין מַפְטִירִין אַחַר הַפֶּסַח אֲפִיקוֹמָן.

רָשָׁע מַה הוּא אוֹמֵר: מָה הָעֲבֹדָה הַזֹּאת לָכֶם. לָכֶם וְלֹא לוֹ. וּלְפִי שֶׁהוֹצִיא אֶת עַצְמוֹ מִן הַכְּלָל כָּפַר בָּעִקָּר. וְאַף אַתָּה הַקְהֵה אֶת שִׁנָּיו, וֶאֱמָר־לוֹ: בַּעֲבוּר זֶה עָשָׂה יְיָ לִי בְּצֵאתִי מִמִּצְרָיִם. לִי וְלֹא לוֹ, אִלּוּ הָיָה שָׁם לֹא הָיָה נִגְאָל.

תָּם מַה הוּא אוֹמֵר: מַה זֹּאת. וְאָמַרְתָּ אֵלָיו: בְּחֹזֶק יָד הוֹצִיאָנוּ יְיָ מִמִּצְרַיִם, מִבֵּית עֲבָדִים.

וְשֶׁאֵינוֹ יוֹדֵעַ לִשְׁאוֹל—אַתְּ פְּתַח לוֹ, שֶׁנֶּאֱמַר: וְהִגַּדְתָּ לְבִנְךָ בַּיּוֹם הַהוּא לֵאמֹר: בַּעֲבוּר זֶה עָשָׂה יְיָ לִי בְּצֵאתִי מִמִּצְרָיִם.

One may possibly think that the explanation of the Passover must start with the beginning of the month of Nisan. To avoid such error, it is written, "On that day." But from the expression, "On that day," one may infer that the explanation should be begun while it is yet day. To avoid this error, it is written, "It is because of this" (meaning the matzah and bitter herbs); it refers to the time when the matzah and the bitter herbs are actually placed before you.

In ancient days, our fathers were idol-worshippers, but now the Eternal has brought us near to worship Him; as it is said: "And Joshua said to all the people: Thus says the Lord, God of Israel: 'Your fathers dwelt in olden times beyond the River, even Terah, the father of Abraham, and the father of Nahor; and they served other gods. And I took your father Abraham from beyond the River, and led him throughout all the land of Canaan, and multiplied his seed, and gave him Isaac. And to Isaac I gave Jacob and Esau; and I gave to Esau Mount Seir to occupy; and Jacob and his children went down into Egypt.'"

יָכוֹל מֵרֹאשׁ חֹדֶשׁ, תַּלְמוּד לוֹמַר: בַּיּוֹם הַהוּא. אִי בַּיּוֹם הַהוּא, יָכֹל מִבְּעוֹד יוֹם, תַּלְמוּד לוֹמַר: בַּעֲבוּר זֶה. בַּעֲבוּר זֶה לֹא אָמַרְתִּי אֶלָּא בְּשָׁעָה שֶׁיֵּשׁ מַצָּה וּמָרוֹר מֻנָּחִים לְפָנֶיךָ.

מִתְּחִלָּה עוֹבְדֵי עֲבוֹדָה זָרָה הָיוּ אֲבוֹתֵינוּ, וְעַכְשָׁו קֵרְבָנוּ הַמָּקוֹם לַעֲבוֹדָתוֹ, שֶׁנֶּאֱמַר: וַיֹּאמֶר יְהוֹשֻׁעַ אֶל כָּל הָעָם, כֹּה אָמַר יְיָ אֱלֹהֵי יִשְׂרָאֵל, בְּעֵבֶר הַנָּהָר יָשְׁבוּ אֲבוֹתֵיכֶם מֵעוֹלָם, תֶּרַח אֲבִי אַבְרָהָם וַאֲבִי נָחוֹר; וַיַּעַבְדוּ אֱלֹהִים אֲחֵרִים. וָאֶקַּח אֶת אֲבִיכֶם אֶת אַבְרָהָם מֵעֵבֶר הַנָּהָר, וָאוֹלֵךְ אוֹתוֹ בְּכָל אֶרֶץ כְּנָעַן; וָאַרְבֶּה אֶת זַרְעוֹ, וָאֶתֵּן לוֹ אֶת יִצְחָק. וָאֶתֵּן לְיִצְחָק אֶת יַעֲקֹב וְאֶת עֵשָׂו; וָאֶתֵּן לְעֵשָׂו אֶת הַר שֵׂעִיר לָרֶשֶׁת אוֹתוֹ, וְיַעֲקֹב וּבָנָיו יָרְדוּ מִצְרָיִם.

מתחלה
עובדי עבודה זרה היו אבותינו
ועכשו קרבנו המקום לעבדתו.

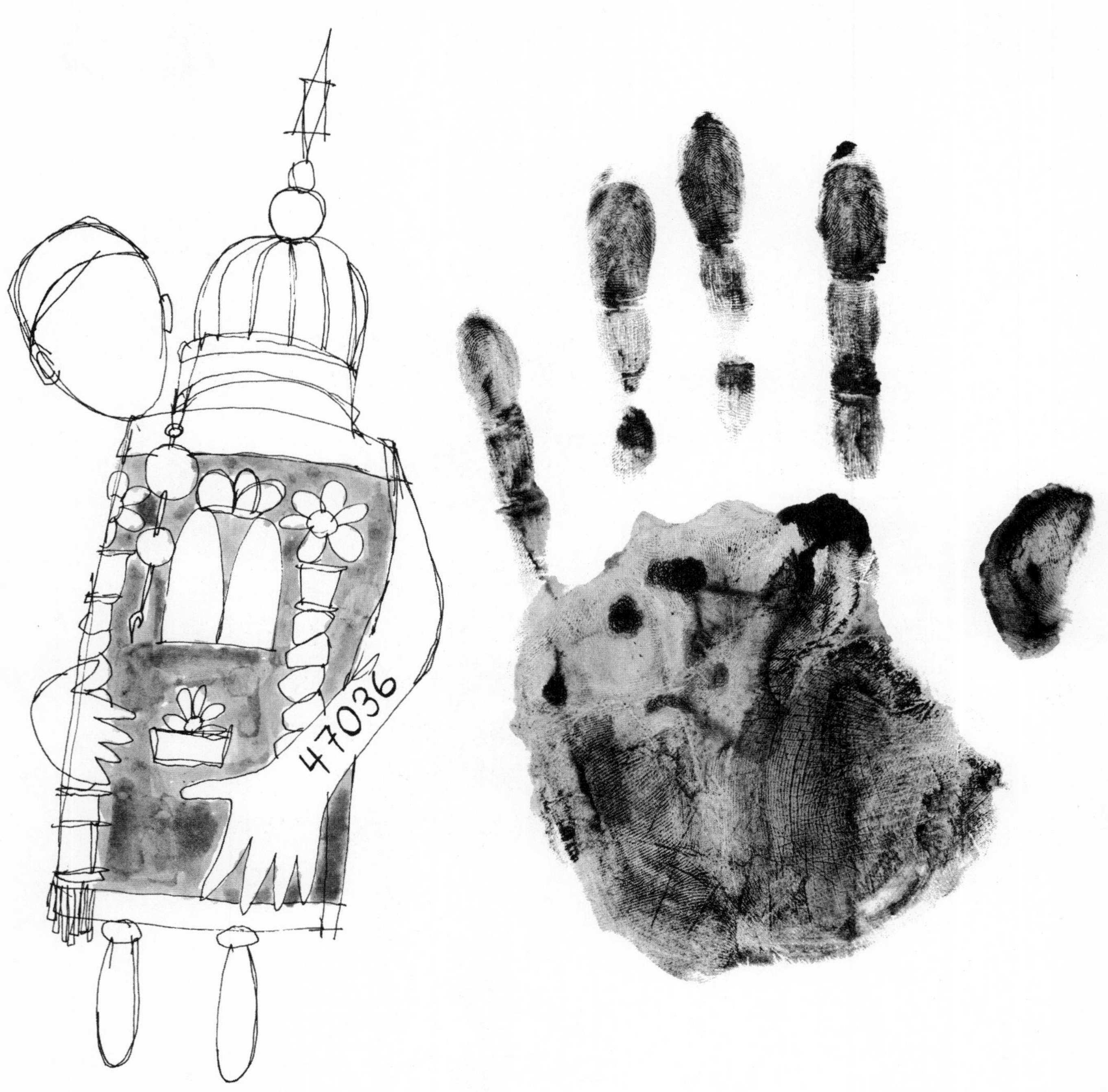
47036

Blessed be He who kept His promise to Israel! Blessed be He! For the Holy One, blessed be He, determined when the Egyptian servitude should end, that He might perform that which He had told our father Abraham when He made His Covenant with him. As it is said: "And He said to Abraham: 'Know for a fact that your children shall be strangers in a foreign land, and shall serve and shall be afflicted for four hundred years; and that nation whom they shall serve, I will judge; and afterwards they shall escape with great wealth.'"

בָּרוּךְ שׁוֹמֵר הַבְטָחָתוֹ לְיִשְׂרָאֵל, בָּרוּךְ הוּא. שֶׁהַקָּדוֹשׁ בָּרוּךְ הוּא חִשַּׁב אֶת הַקֵּץ לַעֲשׂוֹת כְּמוֹ שֶׁאָמַר לְאַבְרָהָם אָבִינוּ בִּבְרִית בֵּין הַבְּתָרִים, שֶׁנֶּאֱמַר: וַיֹּאמֶר לְאַבְרָם, יָדֹעַ תֵּדַע כִּי גֵר יִהְיֶה זַרְעֲךָ בְּאֶרֶץ לֹא לָהֶם, וַעֲבָדוּם וְעִנּוּ אֹתָם, אַרְבַּע מֵאוֹת שָׁנָה. וְגַם אֶת הַגּוֹי אֲשֶׁר יַעֲבֹדוּ דָּן אָנֹכִי; וְאַחֲרֵי כֵן יֵצְאוּ בִּרְכֻשׁ גָּדוֹל.

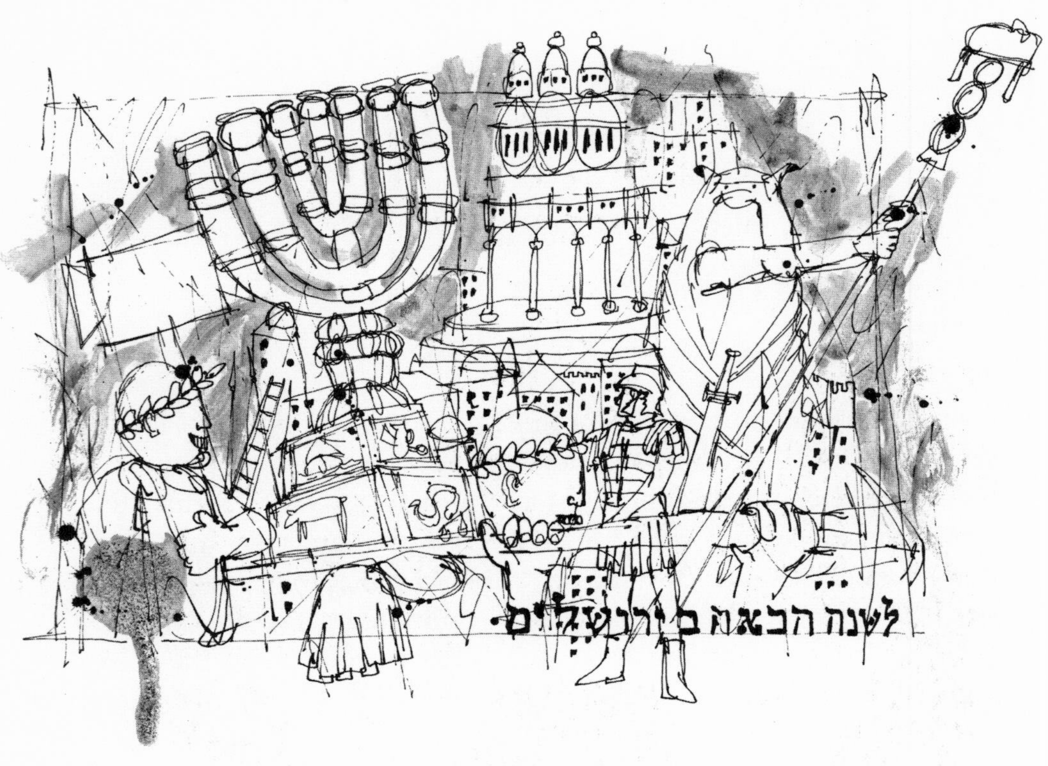

Raise the cup of wine and say:

And this promise has been our fathers' support and ours; for not one tyrant only has risen up against us to destroy us, but in every generation tyrants have sought to destroy us, and the Holy One, blessed be He, has delivered us from their hands.

וְהִיא שֶׁעָמְדָה לַאֲבוֹתֵינוּ וְלָנוּ.
שֶׁלֹּא אֶחָד בִּלְבָד עָמַד עָלֵינוּ לְכַלּוֹתֵנוּ,
אֶלָּא שֶׁבְּכָל דּוֹר וָדוֹר עוֹמְדִים עָלֵינוּ לְכַלּוֹתֵנוּ,
וְהַקָּדוֹשׁ בָּרוּךְ הוּא מַצִּילֵנוּ מִיָּדָם.

והיא שעמדה לאבותינו
ולנו שלא אחד בלבד
עמד עלינו לכלותנו אלא

שבכל דור ודור עומדים
עלינו לכלותנו והקדוש
ברוך הוא מצילנו מידם:

Replace the cup on the table.

Look what Laban, the Syrian, intended to do to our father Jacob. Pharaoh decreed the destruction of the males only, while Laban sought to wipe out the whole family of Jacob; as it is said: "The Syrian would have caused my father Jacob to perish. But he went down into Egypt, and sojourned there few in number, and he became there a nation, great, mighty and populous."

צֵא וּלְמַד מַה בִּקֵּשׁ לָבָן הָאֲרַמִּי לַעֲשׂוֹת לְיַעֲקֹב אָבִינוּ. שֶׁפַּרְעֹה לֹא גָזַר אֶלָּא עַל הַזְּכָרִים, וְלָבָן בִּקֵּשׁ לַעֲקֹר אֶת הַכֹּל, שֶׁנֶּאֱמַר: אֲרַמִּי אֹבֵד אָבִי, וַיֵּרֶד מִצְרַיְמָה, וַיָּגָר שָׁם בִּמְתֵי מְעָט; וַיְהִי שָׁם לְגוֹי גָּדוֹל, עָצוּם וָרָב.

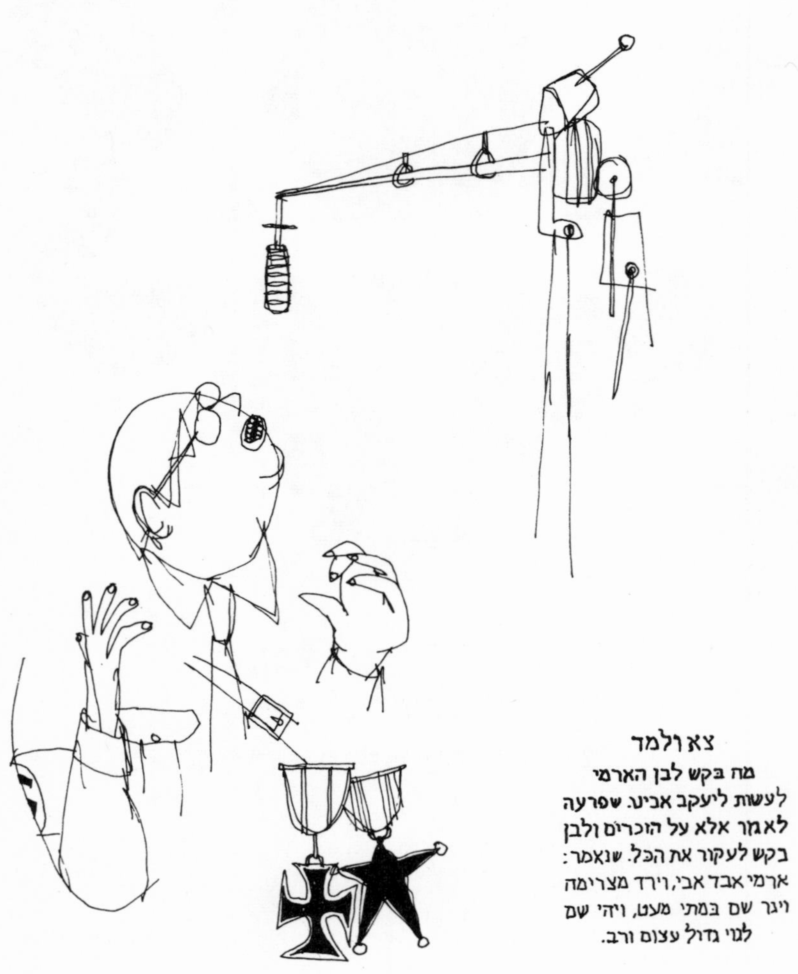
צא ולמד
מה בקש לבן הארמי
לעשות ליעקב אבינו. שפרעה
לא גזר אלא על הזכרים ולבן
בקש לעקור את הכל. שנאמר:
ארמי אבד אבי, וירד מצרימה
ויגר שם במתי מעט, ויהי שם
לגוי גדול עצום ורב.

Just as Laban the Syrian desired to annihilate Jacob and his entire family (whereas Pharaoh issued his decree only against the new-born males), it was the plan of the Nazis to exterminate the entire Jewish population. A comparison can then be drawn between Jacob's flight into Egypt and the flight of many Jews in Eastern Europe to Russia where they sought refuge from the Germans.

And he went down into Egypt; he was compelled (to go) by the word of God. *And he sojourned there*; we infer from this that our father Jacob did not go down with the intention of settling there permanently, but only temporarily; as it is said: "And they said to Pharaoh: 'We have come to live here. There is no pasture for our flocks, for the famine is heavy in the land of Canaan. Now, please, let us dwell in the land of Goshen.'"

וַיֵּרֶד מִצְרַיְמָה, אָנוּס עַל פִּי הַדִּבּוּר. וַיָּגָר שָׁם, מְלַמֵּד שֶׁלֹּא יָרַד יַעֲקֹב אָבִינוּ לְהִשְׁתַּקֵּעַ בְּמִצְרַיִם אֶלָּא לָגוּר שָׁם, שֶׁנֶּאֱמַר: וַיֹּאמְרוּ אֶל פַּרְעֹה, לָגוּר בָּאָרֶץ בָּאנוּ, כִּי אֵין מִרְעֶה לַצֹּאן אֲשֶׁר לַעֲבָדֶיךָ, כִּי כָבֵד הָרָעָב בְּאֶרֶץ כְּנָעַן; וְעַתָּה יֵשְׁבוּ נָא עֲבָדֶיךָ בְּאֶרֶץ גֹּשֶׁן.

במתי מעט — כמו שנאמר:
בשבעים נפש ירדו אבתיך
מצרימה ועתה שמך יי אלהיך
ככוכבי השמים לרב. ויהי שם
לגוי — מלמד שהיו ישראל
מצינים שם גדול, עצום - כמו

Few in number; as it is said: "Your fathers went down into Egypt with seventy persons; and now the Lord our God has made you as numerous as the stars of heaven."

And he became there a nation; from this it may be inferred that the Israelites kept themselves as a distinct nation.

Mighty; as it is written: "And the children of Israel were fruitful, and increased abundantly, and multiplied, and grew exceedingly mighty; and the land was filled with them."

And populous; as it is said: "I caused you to increase as the growth of the field. And you did increase and grow up, and you came to excellent beauty."

בִּמְתֵי מְעָט, כְּמוֹ שֶׁנֶּאֱמַר: בְּשִׁבְעִים נֶפֶשׁ יָרְדוּ אֲבֹתֶיךָ מִצְרָיְמָה; וְעַתָּה שָׂמְךָ יְיָ אֱלֹהֶיךָ כְּכוֹכְבֵי הַשָּׁמַיִם לָרֹב.

וַיְהִי שָׁם לְגוֹי, מְלַמֵּד שֶׁהָיוּ יִשְׂרָאֵל מְצֻיָּנִים שָׁם.

גָּדוֹל עָצוּם, כְּמוֹ שֶׁנֶּאֱמַר: וּבְנֵי יִשְׂרָאֵל פָּרוּ וַיִּשְׁרְצוּ, וַיִּרְבּוּ וַיַּעַצְמוּ בִּמְאֹד מְאֹד; וַתִּמָּלֵא הָאָרֶץ אֹתָם.

וָרָב. כְּמוֹ שֶׁנֶּאֱמַר: רְבָבָה כְּצֶמַח הַשָּׂדֶה נְתַתִּיךְ, וַתִּרְבִּי וַתִּגְדְּלִי, וַתָּבֹאִי בַּעֲדִי עֲדָיִים; שָׁדַיִם נָכֹנוּ, וּשְׂעָרֵךְ צִמֵּחַ, וְאַתְּ עֵרֹם וְעֶרְיָה.

"And the Egyptians mistreated us, and afflicted us, and forced upon us hard labor."

And the Egyptians mistreated us; as it is said: "Come let us outwit them, lest they multiply, and should a war break out, they might join our enemies, and fight against us, and escape."

וַיָּרֵעוּ אֹתָנוּ הַמִּצְרִים, וַיְעַנּוּנוּ; וַיִּתְּנוּ עָלֵינוּ עֲבֹדָה קָשָׁה.

וַיָּרֵעוּ אֹתָנוּ הַמִּצְרִים, כְּמוֹ שֶׁנֶּאֱמַר: הָבָה נִתְחַכְּמָה לוֹ,
פֶּן יִרְבֶּה, וְהָיָה כִּי תִקְרֶאנָה מִלְחָמָה, וְנוֹסַף גַּם הוּא עַל שֹׂנְאֵינוּ
וְנִלְחַם בָּנוּ וְעָלָה מִן הָאָרֶץ.

And afflicted us; as it is said: "And they set over them taskmasters to afflict them with hard labor. And they built for Pharaoh store-cities, Pithom and Raamses."

And forced upon us hard labor; as it is said: "And the Egyptians made the children of Israel serve them with rigor."

"And we cried to the Lord, God of our fathers, and the Lord heard our voice and saw our affliction, our toil and our oppression."

וַיְעַנּֽוּנוּ כְּמוֹ שֶׁנֶּאֱמַר: וַיָּשִֽׂימוּ עָלָיו שָׂרֵי מִסִּים, לְמַֽעַן עַנֹּתוֹ בְּסִבְלֹתָם. וַיִּֽבֶן עָרֵי מִסְכְּנוֹת לְפַרְעֹה, אֶת פִּתֹם וְאֶת רַעַמְסֵס.

וַיִּתְּנוּ עָלֵֽינוּ עֲבֹדָה קָשָׁה, כְּמוֹ שֶׁנֶּאֱמַר: וַיַּעֲבִֽדוּ מִצְרַֽיִם אֶת בְּנֵי יִשְׂרָאֵל בְּפָֽרֶךְ.

וַנִּצְעַק אֶל יְיָ אֱלֹהֵי אֲבֹתֵֽינוּ, וַיִּשְׁמַע יְיָ אֶת קֹלֵֽנוּ, וַיַּרְא אֶת עָנְיֵֽנוּ, וְאֶת עֲמָלֵֽנוּ, וְאֶת לַחֲצֵֽנוּ.

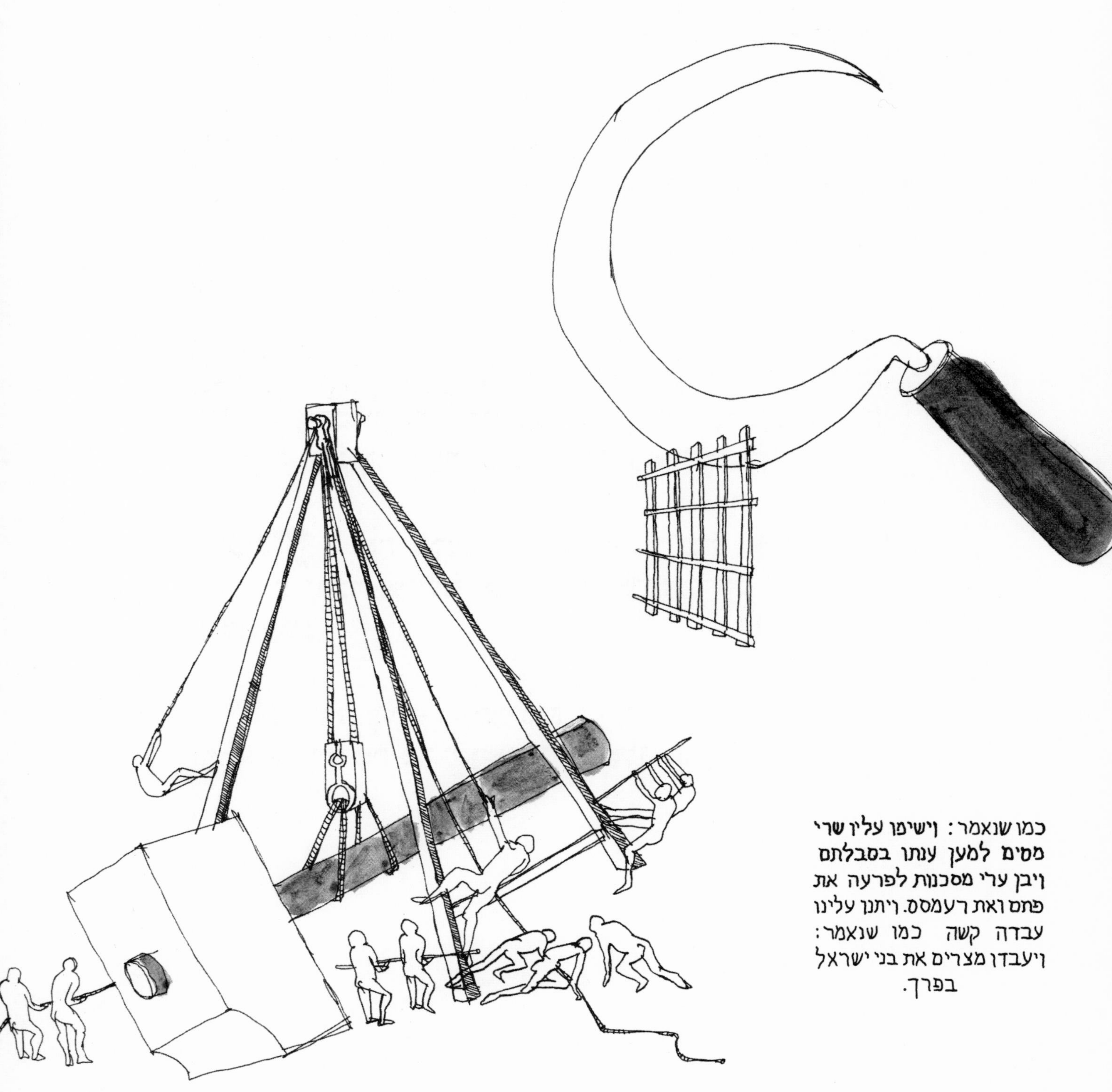

כמו שנאמר: וישימו עליו שרי
מסים למען ענתו בסבלתם
ויבן ערי מסכנות לפרעה את
פתם ואת רעמסס. ויתנו עלינו
עבדה קשה כמו שנאמר:
ויעבדו מצרים את בני ישראל
בפרך.

And we cried to the Lord, God of our fathers; as it is said: "And it came to pass in the course of many days, that the king of Egypt died; and the children of Israel sighed under their slavery; and they cried, and their cry came up to God, on account of their bondage."

And the Lord heard our voice; as it is said: "And God heard their groaning, and God remembered His Covenant with Abraham, with Isaac and with Jacob."

And he saw our affliction; this signifies that they were separated from their families; as it is said: "And God saw the plight of Israel, and He understood."

וַנִּצְעַק אֶל יְיָ אֱלֹהֵי אֲבוֹתֵינוּ, כְּמוֹ שֶׁנֶּאֱמַר: וַיְהִי בַיָּמִים הָרַבִּים הָהֵם, וַיָּמָת מֶלֶךְ מִצְרַיִם, וַיֵּאָנְחוּ בְנֵי יִשְׂרָאֵל מִן הָעֲבֹדָה וַיִּזְעָקוּ; וַתַּעַל שַׁוְעָתָם אֶל הָאֱלֹהִים מִן הָעֲבֹדָה.

וַיִּשְׁמַע יְיָ אֶת קֹלֵנוּ, כְּמוֹ שֶׁנֶּאֱמַר, וַיִּשְׁמַע אֱלֹהִים אֶת נַאֲקָתָם; וַיִּזְכֹּר אֱלֹהִים אֶת בְּרִיתוֹ אֶת אַבְרָהָם, אֶת יִצְחָק וְאֶת יַעֲקֹב.

וַיַּרְא אֶת עָנְיֵנוּ–זוֹ פְּרִישׁוּת דֶּרֶךְ אֶרֶץ, כְּמוֹ שֶׁנֶּאֱמַר: וַיַּרְא אֱלֹהִים אֶת בְּנֵי יִשְׂרָאֵל; וַיֵּדַע אֱלֹהִים.

אנכי
לא יהיה
לא תשא
זכור את
כבד את
ברוך
אתה
יי
אלהינו

And our toil; this refers to the destruction of the male children; as it is said: "Every son that is born, you shall cast into the river, but every daughter you shall allow to live."

וְאֶת עֲמָלֵנוּ–אֵלּוּ הַבָּנִים, כְּמוֹ שֶׁנֶּאֱמַר: כָּל הַבֵּן הַיִּלּוֹד
הַיְאֹרָה תַּשְׁלִיכֻהוּ, וְכָל הַבַּת תְּחַיּוּן.

And our oppression; this denotes its severity; as it is said: "And I have also seen how the Egyptians oppress them."

וְאֶת לַחֲצֵנוּ—זֶה הַדְּחַק, כְּמוֹ שֶׁנֶּאֱמַר: וְגַם רָאִיתִי אֶת הַלַּחַץ אֲשֶׁר מִצְרַיִם לֹחֲצִים אֹתָם.

"And the Lord brought us forth out of Egypt with a mighty hand, with an outstretched arm, with great terror, with signs and with wonders."

וַיּוֹצִאֵנוּ יְיָ מִמִּצְרַיִם בְּיָד חֲזָקָה, וּבִזְרֹעַ נְטוּיָה, וּבְמֹרָא גָּדֹל, וּבְאֹתוֹת, וּבְמֹפְתִים.

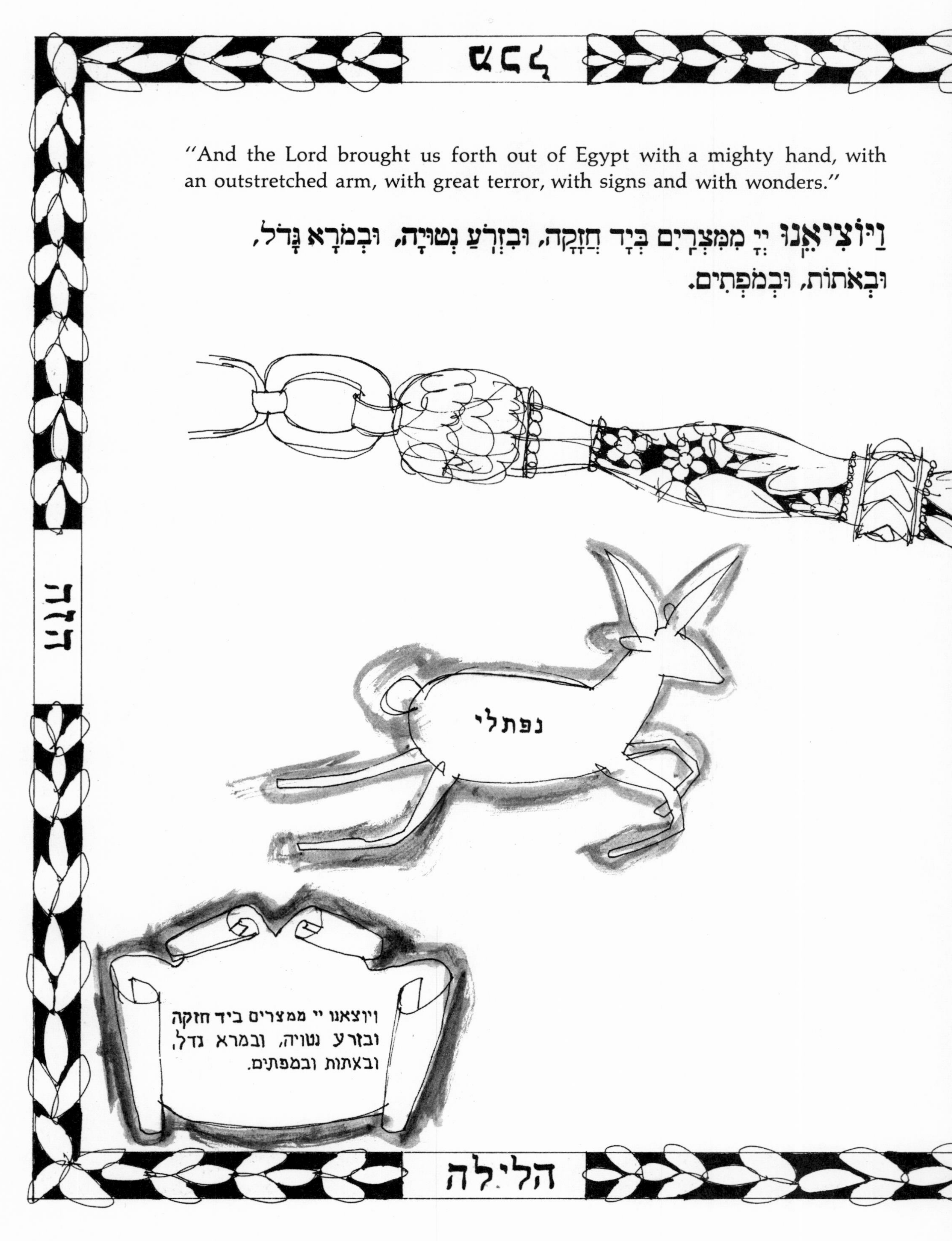
נפתלי
ויוצאנו יי ממצרים ביד חזקה
ובזרע נטויה, ובמרא גדל,
ובאתות ובמפתים.
הלילה

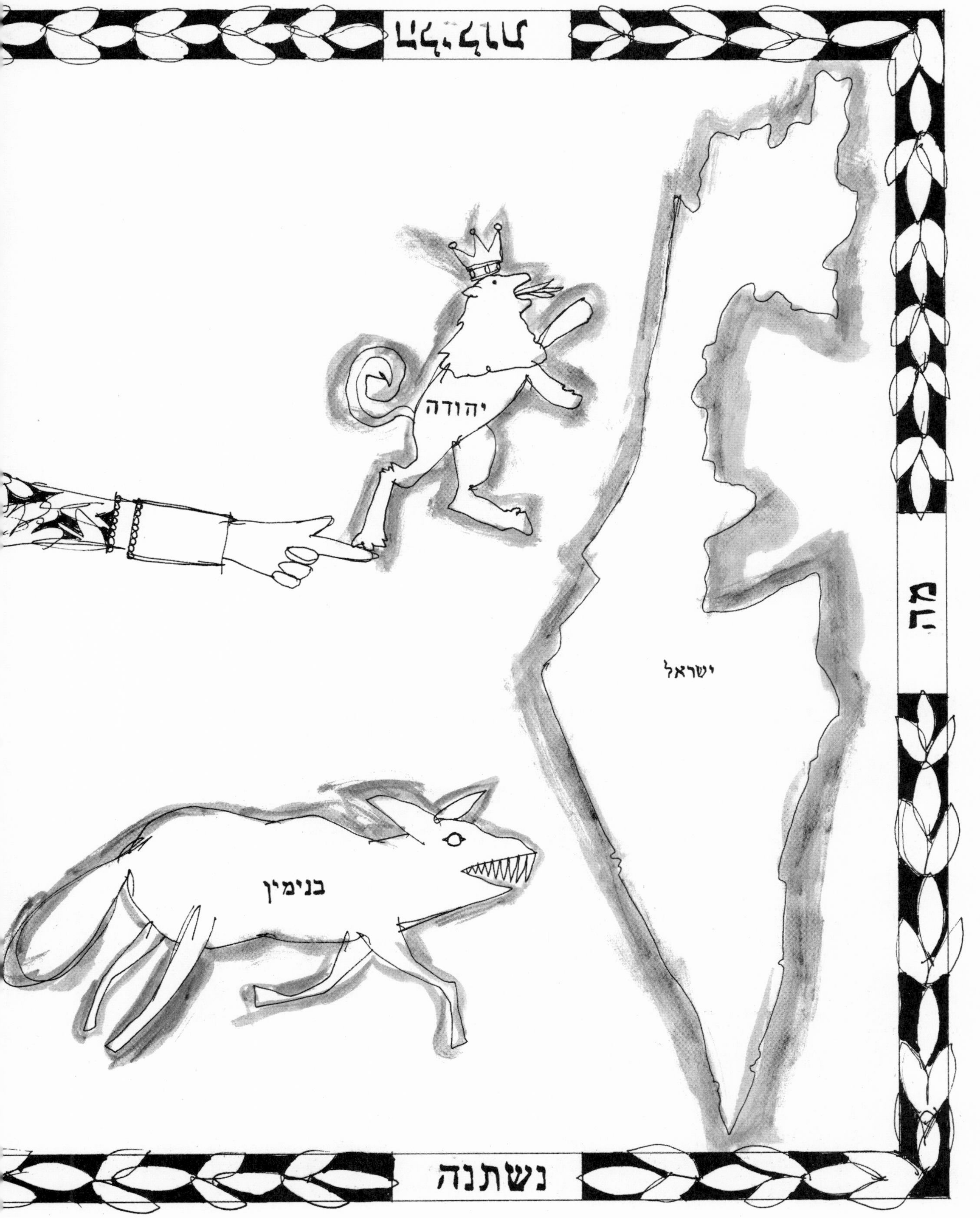
מה
נשתנה
הלילה
יהודה
ישראל
בנימין

And the Lord brought us forth out of Egypt, not by an angel, nor by a seraph, nor by a messenger, but the Holy One, blessed be He, in His own glory and He alone; as it is said: "And I will pass through the land of Egypt this night, and I will smite all the first-born in the land of Fgypt, both man and beasts; and against all the gods of Egypt I will execute judgment; I am the Lord."

And I will pass through the land of Egypt; I, myself, and not an angel. *And I will smite all the first-born;* I, myself, and no seraph. *And against all the gods of Egypt I will execute judgment;* I, myself, and not a messenger. *I am the Lord;* It is I; and none other.

וַיּוֹצִאֵנוּ יְיָ מִמִּצְרַיִם–לֹא עַל יְדֵי מַלְאָךְ, וְלֹא עַל יְדֵי שָׂרָף, וְלֹא עַל יְדֵי שָׁלִיחַ, אֶלָּא הַקָּדוֹשׁ בָּרוּךְ הוּא בִּכְבוֹדוֹ וּבְעַצְמוֹ, שֶׁנֶּאֱמַר: וְעָבַרְתִּי בְאֶרֶץ מִצְרַיִם בַּלַּיְלָה הַזֶּה, וְהִכֵּיתִי כָל בְּכוֹר בְּאֶרֶץ מִצְרַיִם, מֵאָדָם וְעַד בְּהֵמָה; וּבְכָל אֱלֹהֵי מִצְרַיִם אֶעֱשֶׂה שְׁפָטִים, אֲנִי יְיָ.

וְעָבַרְתִּי בְאֶרֶץ מִצְרַיִם בַּלַּיְלָה הַזֶּה, אֲנִי וְלֹא מַלְאָךְ; וְהִכֵּיתִי כָל בְּכוֹר בְּאֶרֶץ מִצְרַיִם, אֲנִי וְלֹא שָׂרָף; וּבְכָל אֱלֹהֵי מִצְרַיִם אֶעֱשֶׂה שְׁפָטִים, אֲנִי וְלֹא הַשָּׁלִיחַ; אֲנִי יְיָ, אֲנִי הוּא וְלֹא אַחֵר.

With a mighty hand; this refers to the pestilence; as it is said: "Behold, the hand of the Lord is upon your cattle which are in the field, upon the horses, upon the asses, upon the camels, upon the herd and upon the flocks; a very grievous pestilence."

בְּיָד חֲזָקָה–זוֹ הַדֶּבֶר, כְּמוֹ שֶׁנֶּאֱמַר: הִנֵּה יַד יְיָ הוֹיָה בְּמִקְנְךָ
אֲשֶׁר בַּשָּׂדֶה, בַּסּוּסִים, בַּחֲמֹרִים, בַּגְּמַלִּים, בַּבָּקָר וּבַצֹּאן,
דֶּבֶר כָּבֵד מְאֹד.

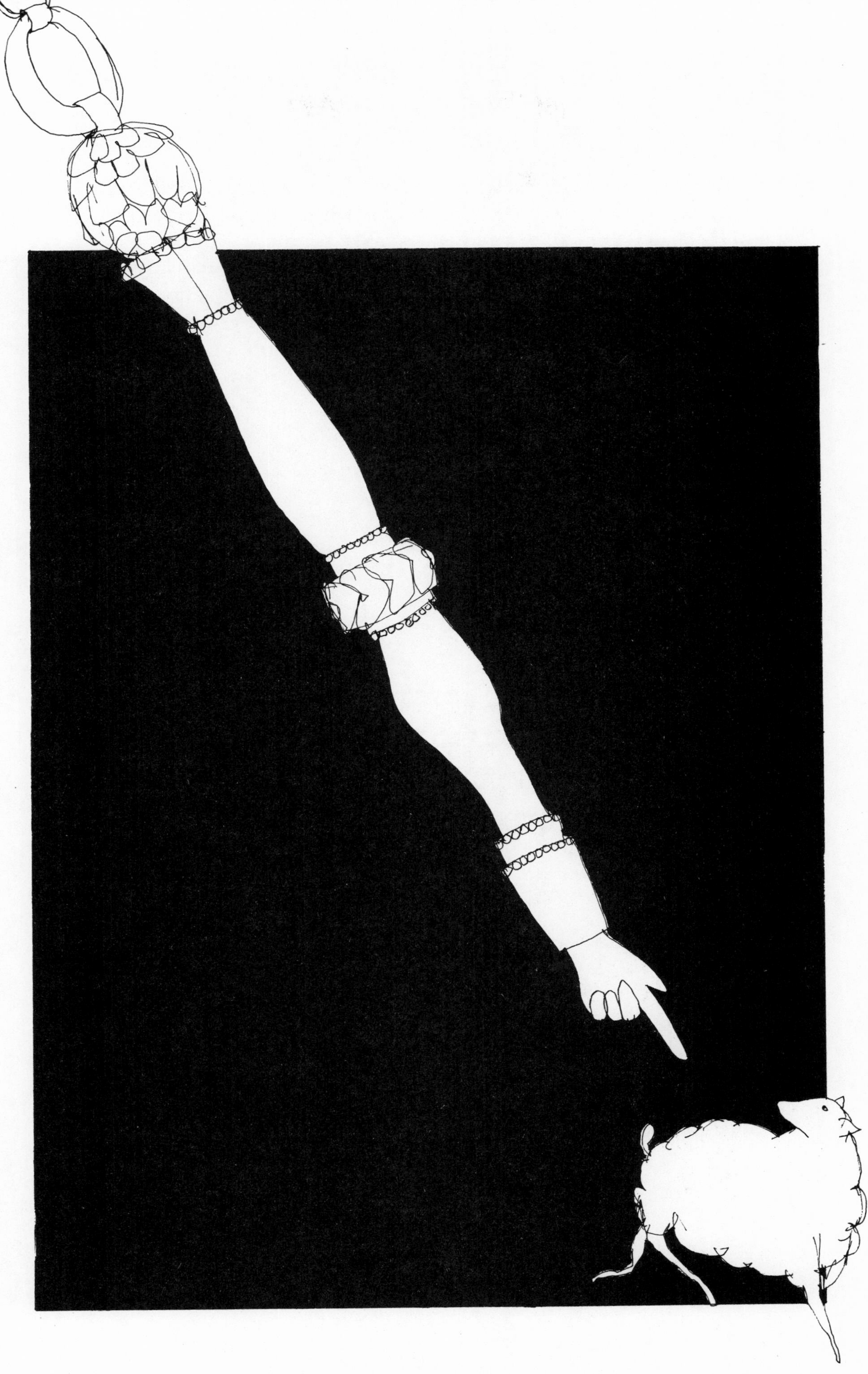

With an outstretched arm; this refers to the sword; as it is said: "Having a drawn sword in His hand, stretched out over Jerusalem."

With great terror; this means the Divine Being revealed Himself; as it is said: "Has any God ever gone and removed a nation from the midst of another nation, by trials, by signs, by wonders, by war, by a mighty hand, by an outstretched arm, and by great terror, as the Lord did for you in Egypt before your eyes."

וּבִזְרֹעַ נְטוּיָה–זוֹ הַחֶרֶב, כְּמוֹ שֶׁנֶּאֱמַר: וְחַרְבּוֹ שְׁלוּפָה בְּיָדוֹ, נְטוּיָה עַל יְרוּשָׁלָיִם.

וּבְמוֹרָא גָּדֹל–זֶה גִּלּוּי שְׁכִינָה, כְּמוֹ שֶׁנֶּאֱמַר: אוֹ הֲנִסָּה אֱלֹהִים לָבוֹא לָקַחַת לוֹ גוֹי מִקֶּרֶב גּוֹי בְּמַסֹּת, בְּאֹתֹת וּבְמוֹפְתִים וּבְמִלְחָמָה, וּבְיָד חֲזָקָה וּבִזְרוֹעַ נְטוּיָה, וּבְמוֹרָאִים גְּדֹלִים, כְּכֹל אֲשֶׁר עָשָׂה לָכֶם יְיָ אֱלֹהֵיכֶם בְּמִצְרַיִם לְעֵינֶיךָ.

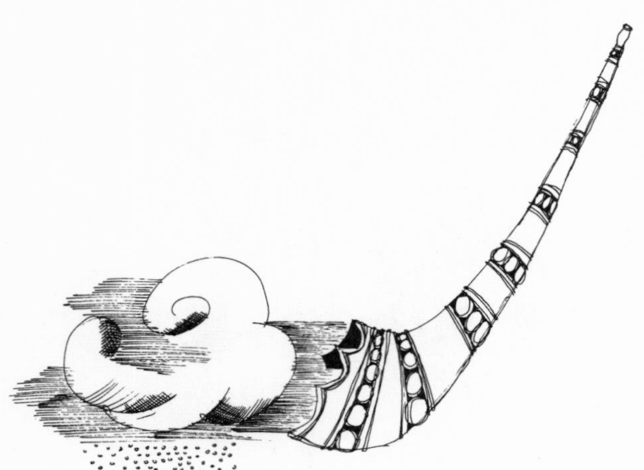

בָּרָד
(HAIL)

With signs; this refers to the miracles performed with the rod; as it is said: "And you shall take this rod in your hand; with it you shall do the signs."

And with wonders; this refers to the plague of blood; as it is said: "And I will show wonders in the heavens and on the earth, blood, fire, and pillars of smoke."

The above verse may also be explained as follows: *With a mighty hand,* denotes two plagues; *with an outstretched arm,* two plagues; *with great terror,* two plagues; *with signs,* two plagues; *and with wonders,* two plagues.

וּבְאֹתוֹת. זֶה הַמַּטֶּה, כְּמוֹ שֶׁנֶּאֱמַר: וְאֶת הַמַּטֶּה הַזֶּה תִּקַּח בְּיָדֶךָ, אֲשֶׁר תַּעֲשֶׂה בּוֹ אֶת הָאֹתֹת.

וּבְמֹפְתִים – זֶה הַדָּם, כְּמוֹ שֶׁנֶּאֱמַר: וְנָתַתִּי מוֹפְתִים בַּשָּׁמַיִם וּבָאָרֶץ:

דָּם, וָאֵשׁ, וְתִמְרוֹת עָשָׁן.

דָּבָר אַחֵר: בְּיָד חֲזָקָה שְׁתַּיִם, וּבִזְרֹעַ נְטוּיָה שְׁתַּיִם, וּבְמֹרָא גָּדֹל שְׁתַּיִם, וּבְאֹתוֹת שְׁתַּיִם, וּבְמֹפְתִים שְׁתַּיִם.

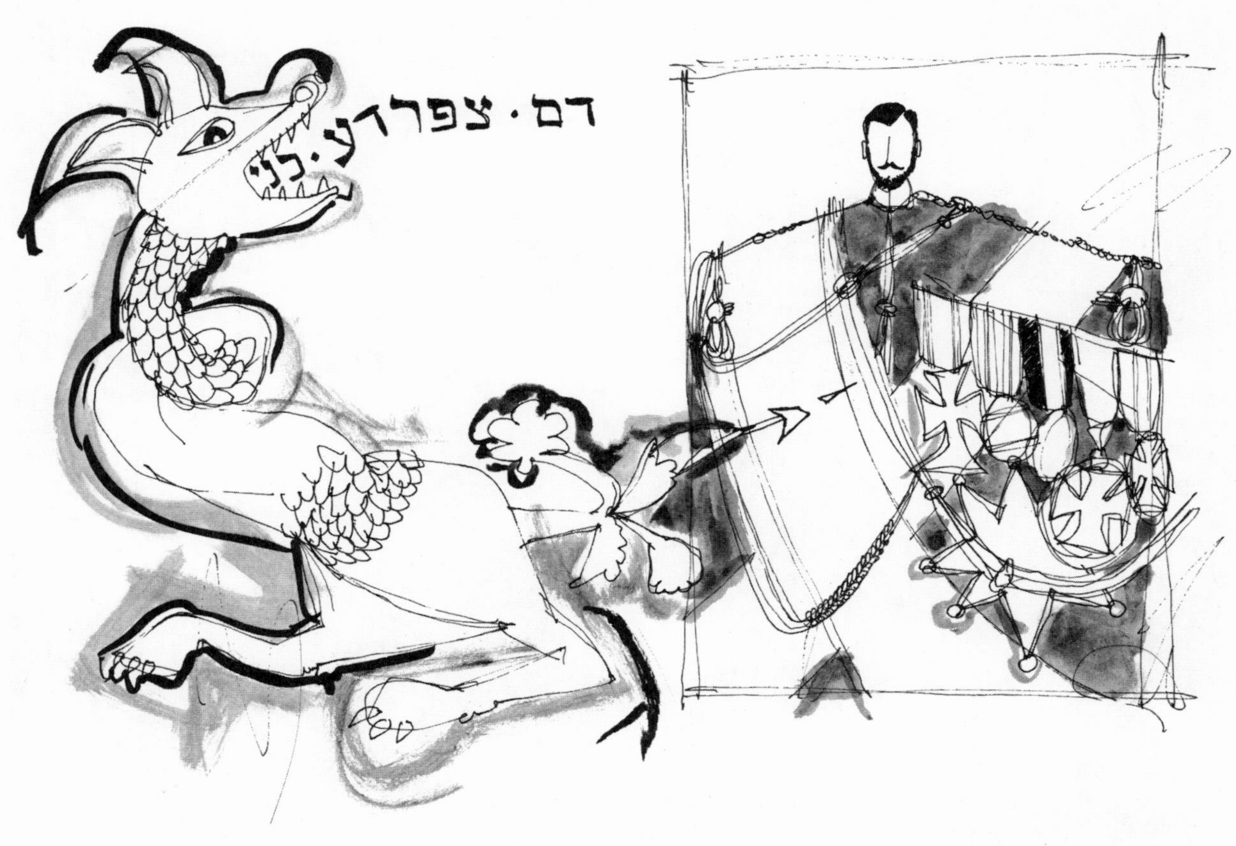
דם · צפרדע · כני

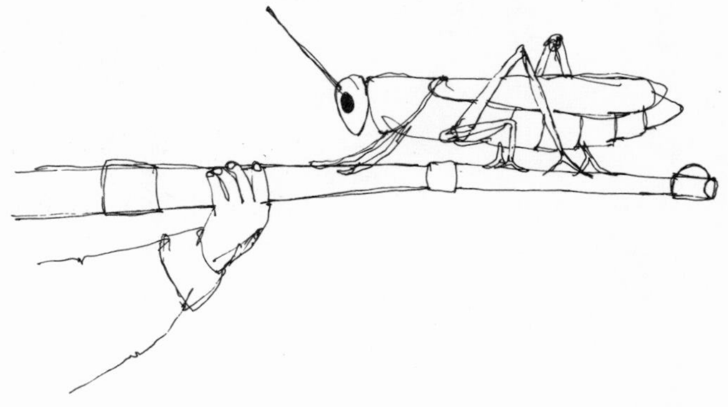

המכות

Spill a drop of wine as each plague is mentioned.

These are the ten plagues which the Holy One, blessed be He, brought upon the Egyptians in Egypt:

BLOOD,
FROGS,
LICE,
BEASTS,
PESTILENCE,

BOILS,
HAIL,
LOCUSTS,
DARKNESS,
SLAYING OF THE FIRST-BORN.

אֵלּוּ עֶשֶׂר מַכּוֹת שֶׁהֵבִיא הַקָּדוֹשׁ בָּרוּךְ הוּא עַל הַמִּצְרִים בְּמִצְרַיִם, וְאֵלּוּ הֵן:

דָּם,
צְפַרְדֵּעַ,
כִּנִּים,
עָרוֹב,
דֶּבֶר,

שְׁחִין,
בָּרָד,
אַרְבֶּה,
חֹשֶׁךְ,
מַכַּת בְּכוֹרוֹת.

Rabbi Judah made mnemonic signs of the initials of the ten plagues:

רַבִּי יְהוּדָה הָיָה נוֹתֵן בָּהֶם סִמָּנִים:

Three drops of wine are spilt.

דְּצַ"ךְ, עֲדַ"שׁ, בְּאַחַ"ב.

Rabbi Yosay, the Galilean, said: "How can you infer that the Egyptians were afflicted with ten plagues in Egypt, and on the sea with fifty plagues? Concerning the ten plagues in Egypt, it is said: "And the magicians said to Pharaoh: 'This is the *finger* of God' but concerning the sea, it is said: 'And Israel saw the mighty *hand with which the* Lord smote the Egyptians, and the people feared the Lord, and believed in the Lord and in His servant Moses.' Now, if by the *finger* they were afflicted with ten plagues, you can infer from this that in Egypt (where the word *finger* is used) they were smitten with ten plagues, and at the sea (where the word *hand* is used) they were smitten with fifty plagues."

רַבִּי יוֹסֵי הַגְּלִילִי אוֹמֵר: מִנַּיִן אַתָּה אוֹמֵר שֶׁלָּקוּ הַמִּצְרִים בְּמִצְרַיִם עֶשֶׂר מַכּוֹת, וְעַל הַיָּם לָקוּ חֲמִשִּׁים מַכּוֹת. בְּמִצְרַיִם מַה הוּא אוֹמֵר: וַיֹּאמְרוּ הַחַרְטֻמִּם אֶל פַּרְעֹה, אֶצְבַּע אֱלֹהִים הִיא. וְעַל הַיָּם מַה הוּא אוֹמֵר: וַיַּרְא יִשְׂרָאֵל אֶת הַיָּד הַגְּדוֹלָה אֲשֶׁר עָשָׂה יְיָ בְּמִצְרַיִם, וַיִּירְאוּ הָעָם אֶת יְיָ; וַיַּאֲמִינוּ בַּייָ וּבְמֹשֶׁה עַבְדּוֹ. כַּמָּה לָקוּ בְּאֶצְבַּע, עֶשֶׂר מַכּוֹת. אֱמוֹר מֵעַתָּה: בְּמִצְרַיִם לָקוּ עֶשֶׂר מַכּוֹת, וְעַל הַיָּם לָקוּ חֲמִשִּׁים מַכּוֹת.

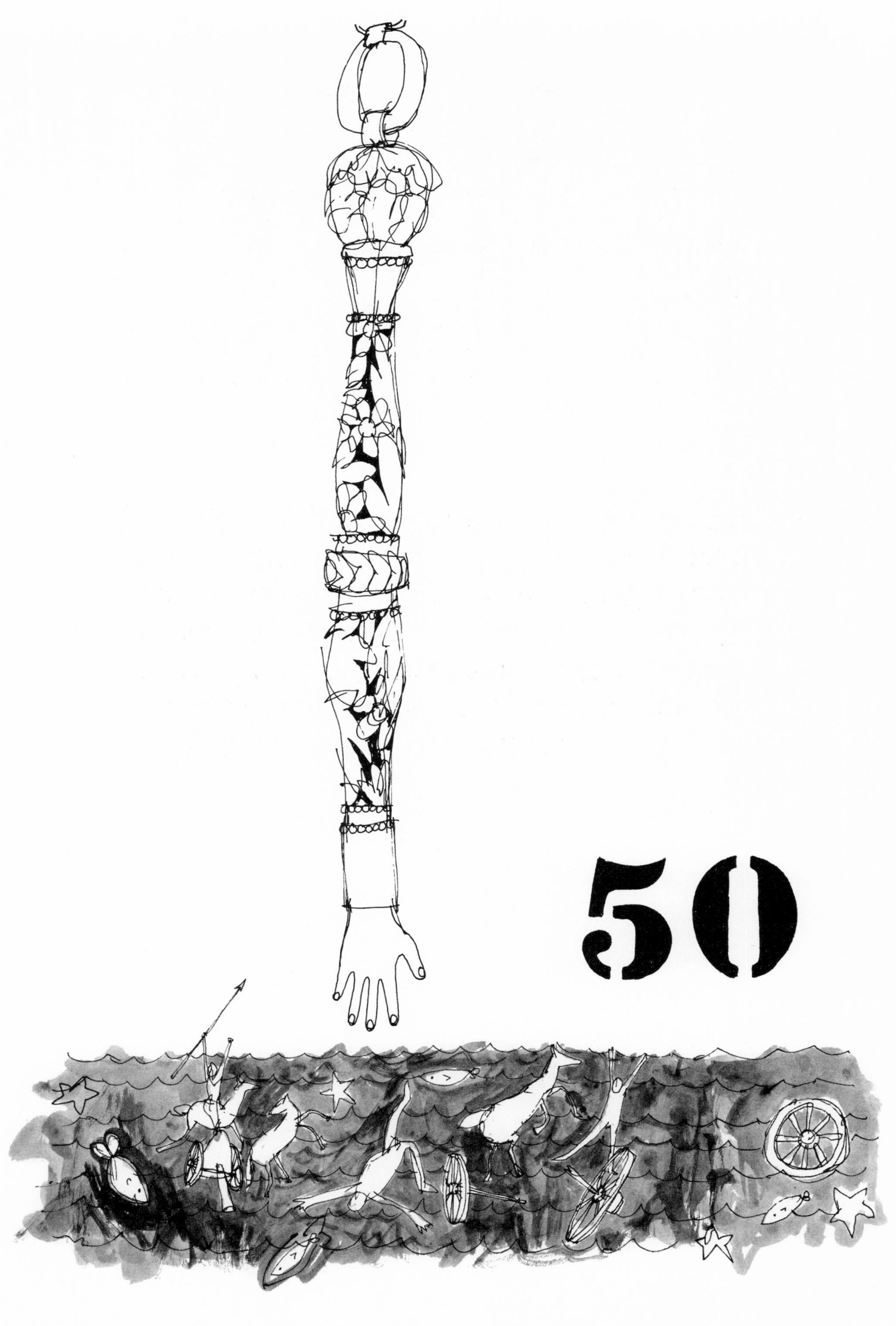
50

Rabbi Eliezer said: "How can it be proven that every plague which the Holy One, blessed be He, brought upon the Egyptians in Egypt consisted of four different plagues? It is said: 'He sent forth upon them the fierceness of his anger, wrath, indignation, trouble, and messengers of evil.' Now, *wrath* denotes one plague; *indignation*, two; *trouble*, three; *and messengers of evil*, four. Therefore, in Egypt they were smitten with forty plagues, and at sea with two hundred plagues."

רַבִּי אֱלִיעֶזֶר אוֹמֵר: מִנַּיִן שֶׁכָּל מַכָּה וּמַכָּה, שֶׁהֵבִיא הַקָּדוֹשׁ בָּרוּךְ הוּא עַל הַמִּצְרִים בְּמִצְרַיִם, הָיְתָה שֶׁל אַרְבַּע מַכּוֹת, שֶׁנֶּאֱמַר: יְשַׁלַּח בָּם חֲרוֹן אַפּוֹ, עֶבְרָה, וָזַעַם, וְצָרָה, מִשְׁלַחַת מַלְאֲכֵי רָעִים. עֶבְרָה אַחַת, וָזַעַם שְׁתַּיִם, וְצָרָה שָׁלֹשׁ, מִשְׁלַחַת מַלְאֲכֵי רָעִים אַרְבַּע. אֱמוֹר מֵעַתָּה: בְּמִצְרַיִם לָקוּ אַרְבָּעִים מַכּוֹת, וְעַל הַיָּם לָקוּ מָאתַיִם מַכּוֹת.

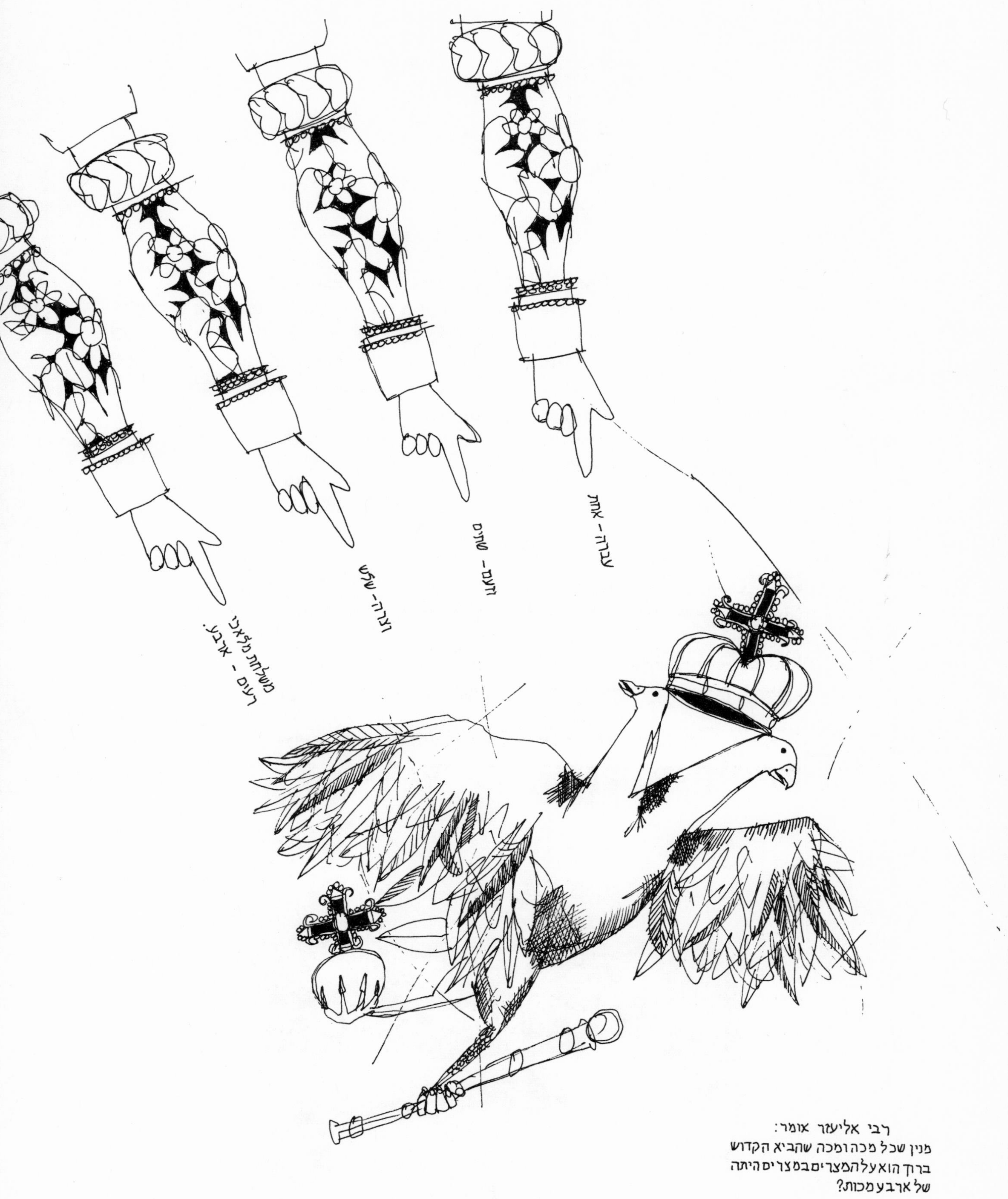

רבי אליעזר אומר:
מנין שכל מכה ומכה שהביא הקדוש
ברוך הוא על המצרים במצרים היתה
של ארבע מכות?

Rabbi Akiba said: "How can it be inferred that every plague which the Holy One, blessed be He, brought upon the Egyptians in Egypt consisted of five plagues? It is said: 'He sent forth upon them the fierceness of his anger, wrath, indignation, trouble, and messengers of evil.' Now, *fierceness of his anger*, denotes one plague; *Wrath*, two; *indignation*, three; *trouble*, four; *messengers of evil*, five. Therefore, in Egypt they were smitten with fifty plagues, and at the sea with two hundred and fifty plagues."

רַבִּי עֲקִיבָא אוֹמֵר: מִנַּיִן שֶׁכָּל מַכָּה וּמַכָּה, שֶׁהֵבִיא הַקָּדוֹשׁ
בָּרוּךְ הוּא עַל הַמִּצְרִים בְּמִצְרַיִם, הָיְתָה שֶׁל חָמֵשׁ מַכּוֹת,
שֶׁנֶּאֱמַר: יְשַׁלַּח בָּם חֲרוֹן אַפּוֹ, עֶבְרָה, וָזַעַם, וְצָרָה, מִשְׁלַחַת
מַלְאֲכֵי רָעִים. חֲרוֹן אַפּוֹ אַחַת, עֶבְרָה שְׁתַּיִם, וָזַעַם שָׁלֹשׁ,
וְצָרָה אַרְבַּע, מִשְׁלַחַת מַלְאֲכֵי רָעִים חָמֵשׁ. אֱמוֹר מֵעַתָּה:
בְּמִצְרַיִם לָקוּ חֲמִשִּׁים מַכּוֹת, וְעַל הַיָּם לָקוּ חֲמִשִּׁים וּמָאתַיִם
מַכּוֹת.

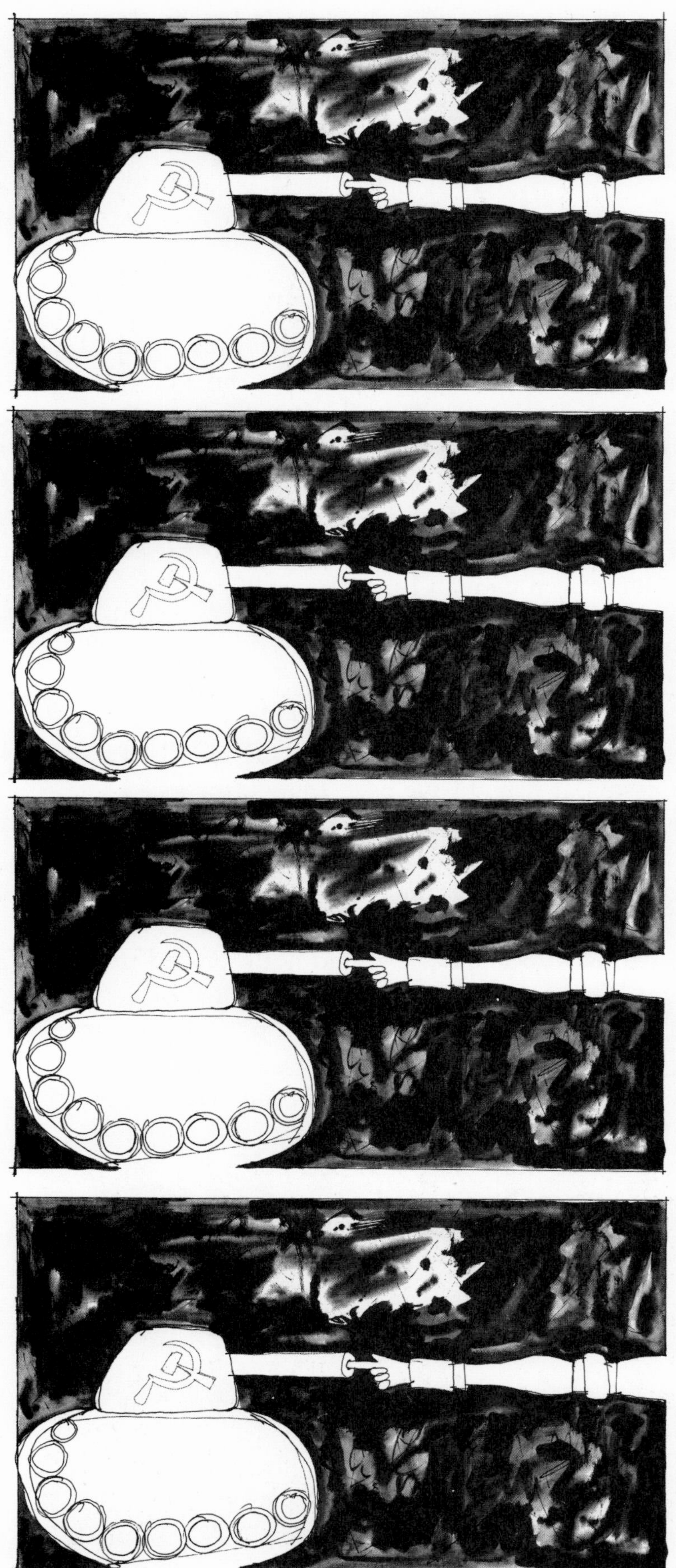

How many are the good deeds the Eternal has done us!

Had He brought us out of Egypt, and had not executed judgment upon the Egyptians, it would have been enough for us.

Had He executed judgment upon the Egyptians, and not upon their gods, it would have been enough for us.

Had He executed judgment upon their gods, and had not slain their first-born, it would have been enough for us.

Had He slain their first-born, and had not given us their wealth, it would have been enough for us.

Had He given us their wealth, and had not divided the sea for us, it would have been enough for us.

Had He divided the sea for us, and had not permitted us to cross on dry land, it would have been enough for us.

Had He permitted us to cross on dry land, and had not drowned our oppressors, it would have been enough for us.

Had He drowned our oppressors, and had not provided for us in the wilderness forty years, it would have been enough for us.

Had He provided for us in the wilderness forty years, and had not fed us with manna, it would have been enough for us.

Had He fed us with manna, and had not ordained the Sabbath, it would have been enough for us.

Had He ordained the Sabbath, and had not brought us to Mount Sinai, it would have been enough for us.

Had He brought us to Mount Sinai, and had not given us the Torah, it would have been enough for us.

Had He given us the Torah, and had not led us into the land of Israel, it would have been enough for us.

Had He brought us into the land of Israel, and had not built for us the Temple, it would have been enough for us.

כַּמָּה מַעֲלוֹת טוֹבוֹת לַמָּקוֹם עָלֵֽינוּ:

אִלּוּ הוֹצִיאָֽנוּ מִמִּצְרַֽיִם, וְלֹא עָשָׂה בָהֶם שְׁפָטִים, דַּיֵּֽנוּ.

אִלּוּ עָשָׂה בָהֶם שְׁפָטִים, וְלֹא עָשָׂה בֵאלֹהֵיהֶם, דַּיֵּֽנוּ.

אִלּוּ עָשָׂה בֵאלֹהֵיהֶם, וְלֹא הָרַג אֶת בְּכוֹרֵיהֶם, דַּיֵּֽנוּ.

אִלּוּ הָרַג אֶת בְּכוֹרֵיהֶם, וְלֹא נָֽתַן לָֽנוּ אֶת מָמוֹנָם, דַּיֵּֽנוּ.

אִלּוּ נָֽתַן לָֽנוּ אֶת מָמוֹנָם, וְלֹא קָֽרַע לָֽנוּ אֶת הַיָּם, דַּיֵּֽנוּ.

אִלּוּ קָֽרַע לָֽנוּ אֶת הַיָּם, וְלֹא הֶעֱבִירָֽנוּ בְתוֹכוֹ בֶּחָרָבָה, דַּיֵּֽנוּ.

אִלּוּ הֶעֱבִירָֽנוּ בְתוֹכוֹ בֶּחָרָבָה, וְלֹא שִׁקַּע צָרֵֽינוּ בְּתוֹכוֹ, דַּיֵּֽנוּ.

אִלּוּ שִׁקַּע צָרֵֽינוּ בְּתוֹכוֹ, וְלֹא סִפֵּק צָרְכֵּֽנוּ
בַּמִּדְבָּר אַרְבָּעִים שָׁנָה, דַּיֵּֽנוּ.

אִלּוּ סִפֵּק צָרְכֵּֽנוּ בַּמִּדְבָּר אַרְבָּעִים שָׁנָה, וְלֹא
הֶאֱכִילָֽנוּ אֶת הַמָּן, דַּיֵּֽנוּ.

אִלּוּ הֶאֱכִילָֽנוּ אֶת הַמָּן, וְלֹא נָֽתַן לָֽנוּ אֶת הַשַּׁבָּת, דַּיֵּֽנוּ.

אִלּוּ נָֽתַן לָֽנוּ אֶת הַשַּׁבָּת, וְלֹא קֵרְבָֽנוּ לִפְנֵי הַר סִינַי, דַּיֵּֽנוּ.

אִלּוּ קֵרְבָֽנוּ לִפְנֵי הַר סִינַי, וְלֹא נָֽתַן לָֽנוּ אֶת הַתּוֹרָה, דַּיֵּֽנוּ.

אִלּוּ נָֽתַן לָֽנוּ אֶת הַתּוֹרָה, וְלֹא הִכְנִיסָֽנוּ לְאֶֽרֶץ יִשְׂרָאֵל, דַּיֵּֽנוּ.

אִלּוּ הִכְנִיסָֽנוּ לְאֶֽרֶץ יִשְׂרָאֵל, וְלֹא בָֽנָה לָֽנוּ
אֶת בֵּית הַבְּחִירָה, דַּיֵּֽנוּ.

How much more then are we to be grateful for the manifold favors the Eternal has bestowed upon us? He brought us out of Egypt, He executed judgment upon the Egyptians and upon their gods, He slew their first-born, He gave us their wealth, He divided for us the sea, He permitted us to cross on dry land, He drowned our oppressors, He provided for us in the wilderness forty years, He fed us with manna, He ordained the Sabbath, He brought us to Mount Sinai, He gave us the Torah, He led us into the land of Israel, and He built for us the Temple to make atonement for all our sins.

עַל אַחַת כַּמָּה וְכַמָּה, טוֹבָה כְּפוּלָה וּמְכֻפֶּלֶת לַמָּקוֹם עָלֵינוּ: שֶׁהוֹצִיאָנוּ מִמִּצְרַיִם, וְעָשָׂה בָהֶם שְׁפָטִים, וְעָשָׂה בֵאלֹהֵיהֶם, וְהָרַג אֶת בְּכוֹרֵיהֶם, וְנָתַן לָנוּ אֶת מָמוֹנָם, וְקָרַע לָנוּ אֶת הַיָּם, וְהֶעֱבִירָנוּ בְתוֹכוֹ בֶּחָרָבָה, וְשִׁקַּע צָרֵינוּ בְּתוֹכוֹ, וְסִפֵּק צָרְכֵּנוּ בַּמִּדְבָּר אַרְבָּעִים שָׁנָה, וְהֶאֱכִילָנוּ אֶת הַמָּן, וְנָתַן לָנוּ אֶת הַשַּׁבָּת, וְקֵרְבָנוּ לִפְנֵי הַר סִינַי, וְנָתַן לָנוּ אֶת הַתּוֹרָה, וְהִכְנִיסָנוּ לְאֶרֶץ יִשְׂרָאֵל, וּבָנָה לָנוּ אֶת בֵּית הַבְּחִירָה לְכַפֵּר עַל כָּל עֲוֹנוֹתֵינוּ.

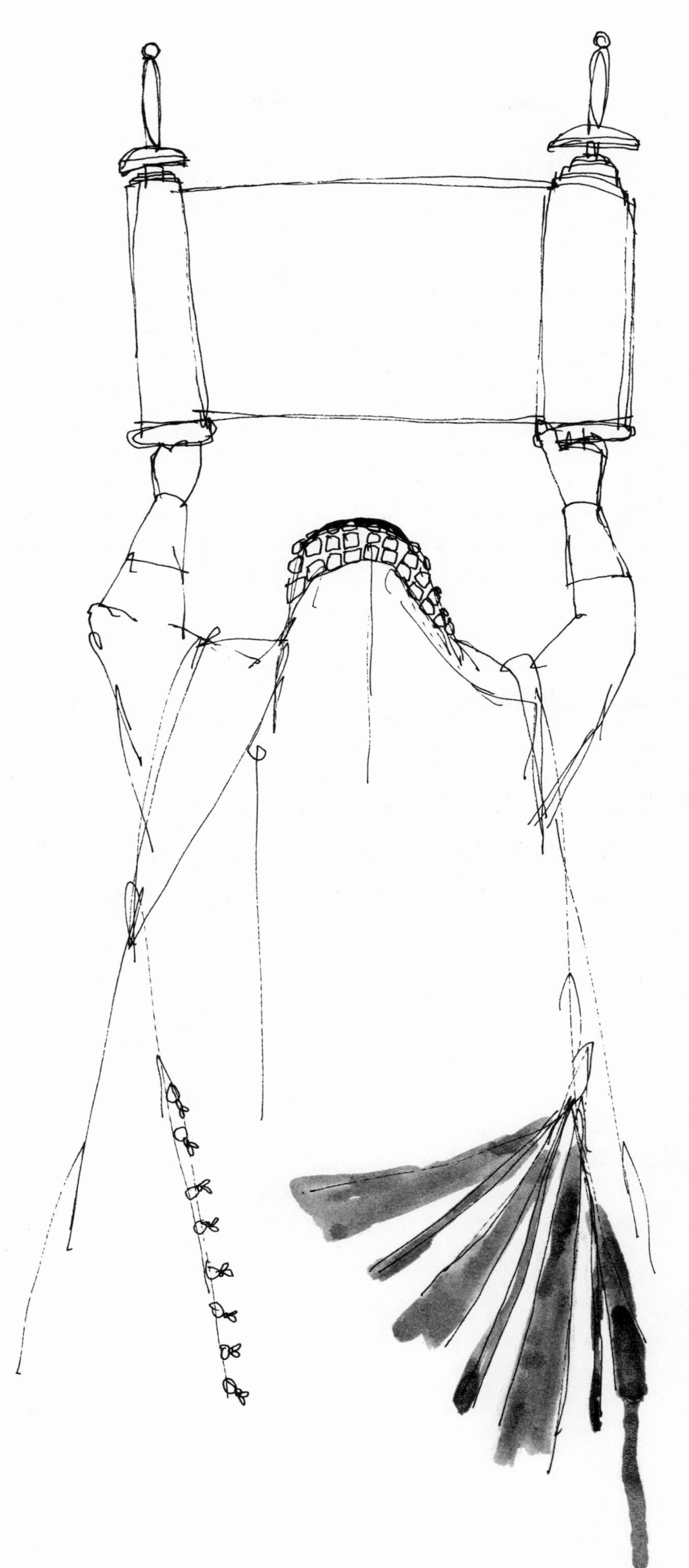

Rabban Gamaliel said: "Whoever does not mention the meaning of these three symbols, the paschal lamb, the unleavened bread, and the bitter herbs, has not fulfilled his obligation."

The leader points to the roasted bone which is symbolic of the paschal lamb, and recites:

Why did our fathers eat the paschal lamb while the Temple was still in existence? Because the Holy One, blessed be He, passed over our fathers' house in Egypt; as it is said: "And you shall say: 'It is the Lord's Passover, because He passed over the house of the children of Israel in Egypt, when He smote the first-born of the Egyptians, and He spared our houses.' And the people bowed their heads and worshipped."

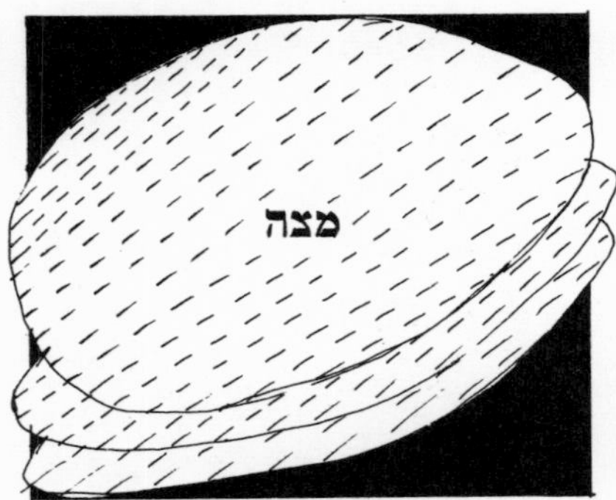

The leader points to the matzah and says:

Why do we eat this unleavened bread? Because there was not enough time for the dough of our fathers to rise before the Supreme King of Kings, the Holy One, blessed be He, appeared to them and redeemed them; as it is said: "And they baked unleavened cakes of the dough which they brought forth out of Egypt for it had not risen; because they were driven out of Egypt and could not tarry; neither had they prepared for themselves any food."

The leader points to the bitter herbs and says:

Why do we eat these bitter herbs? Because the Egyptians embittered the lives of our fathers in Egypt; as it is said: 'And they embittered their lives with hard labor in mortar and in brick, and in all manner of work in the field; all their labor was imposed upon them with rigor."

רַבָּן גַּמְלִיאֵל הָיָה אוֹמֵר: כָּל שֶׁלֹּא אָמַר שְׁלשָׁה דְבָרִים אֵלּוּ בַּפֶּסַח לֹא יָצָא יְדֵי חוֹבָתוֹ, וְאֵלּוּ הֵן:

פֶּסַח, מַצָּה, וּמָרוֹר.

פֶּסַח, שֶׁהָיוּ אֲבוֹתֵינוּ אוֹכְלִים בִּזְמַן שֶׁבֵּית הַמִּקְדָּשׁ קַיָּם, עַל שׁוּם מָה. עַל שׁוּם שֶׁפָּסַח הַקָּדוֹשׁ בָּרוּךְ הוּא עַל בָּתֵּי אֲבוֹתֵינוּ בְּמִצְרָיִם, שֶׁנֶּאֱמַר: וַאֲמַרְתֶּם זֶבַח פֶּסַח הוּא לַיָי, אֲשֶׁר פָּסַח עַל בָּתֵּי בְנֵי יִשְׂרָאֵל בְּמִצְרַיִם בְּנָגְפּוֹ אֶת מִצְרַיִם, וְאֶת בָּתֵּינוּ הִצִּיל; וַיִּקֹּד הָעָם וַיִּשְׁתַּחֲווּ.

מַצָּה זוֹ, שֶׁאָנוּ אוֹכְלִים, עַל שׁוּם מָה. עַל שׁוּם שֶׁלֹּא הִסְפִּיק בְּצֵקָם שֶׁל אֲבוֹתֵינוּ לְהַחֲמִיץ עַד שֶׁנִּגְלָה עֲלֵיהֶם מֶלֶךְ מַלְכֵי הַמְּלָכִים, הַקָּדוֹשׁ בָּרוּךְ הוּא, וּגְאָלָם, שֶׁנֶּאֱמַר: וַיֹּאפוּ אֶת הַבָּצֵק אֲשֶׁר הוֹצִיאוּ מִמִּצְרַיִם, עֻגֹת מַצּוֹת כִּי לֹא חָמֵץ; כִּי גֹרְשׁוּ מִמִּצְרַיִם, וְלֹא יָכְלוּ לְהִתְמַהְמֵהַּ, וְגַם צֵדָה לֹא עָשׂוּ לָהֶם.

מָרוֹר זֶה, שֶׁאָנוּ אוֹכְלִים, עַל שׁוּם מָה. עַל שׁוּם שֶׁמֵּרְרוּ הַמִּצְרִים אֶת חַיֵּי אֲבוֹתֵינוּ בְּמִצְרַיִם, שֶׁנֶּאֱמַר: וַיְמָרְרוּ אֶת חַיֵּיהֶם בַּעֲבֹדָה קָשָׁה, בְּחֹמֶר וּבִלְבֵנִים, וּבְכָל עֲבֹדָה בַּשָּׂדֶה; אֵת כָּל עֲבֹדָתָם אֲשֶׁר עָבְדוּ בָהֶם בְּפָרֶךְ.

In every generation, every Jew must regard himself as though he, personally, were brought out of Egypt; as it is said: "And you shall tell your son on that day, saying: It is because of what the Lord did for *me* when I left Egypt'." It was not our ancestors alone that the Holy One, blessed be He, redeemed from Egypt, but He redeemed us with them; as it is said: "And He brought *us* out of there, that He might bring *us* into the land which He had promised to our fathers."

בְּכָל דּוֹר וָדוֹר חַיָּב אָדָם לִרְאוֹת אֶת עַצְמוֹ כְּאִלּוּ הוּא יָצָא מִמִּצְרָיִם, שֶׁנֶּאֱמַר: וְהִגַּדְתָּ לְבִנְךָ בַּיּוֹם הַהוּא לֵאמֹר: בַּעֲבוּר זֶה עָשָׂה יְיָ לִי בְּצֵאתִי מִמִּצְרָיִם. לֹא אֶת אֲבוֹתֵינוּ בִּלְבָד גָּאַל הַקָּדוֹשׁ בָּרוּךְ הוּא, אֶלָּא אַף אוֹתָנוּ גָּאַל עִמָּהֶם, שֶׁנֶּאֱמַר: וְאוֹתָנוּ הוֹצִיא מִשָּׁם, לְמַעַן הָבִיא אֹתָנוּ, לָתֶת לָנוּ אֶת הָאָרֶץ אֲשֶׁר נִשְׁבַּע לַאֲבֹתֵינוּ.

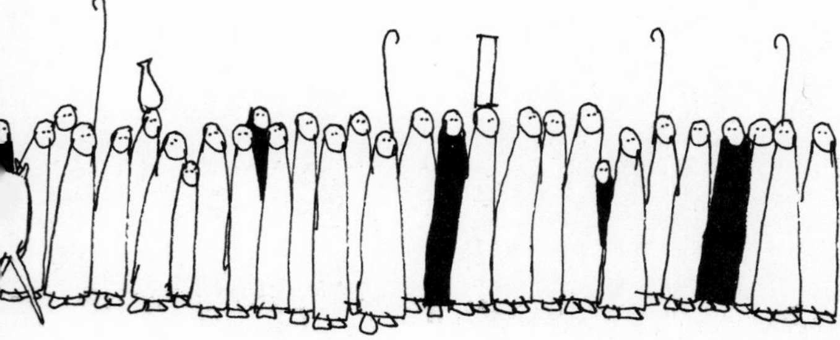

Raise the cup of wine and recite:

Therefore it our duty to thank, praise, laud, glorify, extol, honor, bless, exalt and adore Him, who performed all these miracles for our ancestors and for us. He brought us from slavery to freedom, from sorrow to joy, from mourning to festive gladness, from darkness to daylight, and from servitude to redemption. Therefore let us chant to Him a new song: Hallelujah.

Replace the cup of wine on the table.

לְפִיכָךְ: אֲנַחְנוּ חַיָּבִים לְהוֹדוֹת, לְהַלֵּל, לְשַׁבֵּחַ, לְפָאֵר,
לְרוֹמֵם, לְהַדֵּר, לְבָרֵךְ, לְעַלֵּה וּלְקַלֵּס לְמִי שֶׁעָשָׂה לַאֲבוֹתֵינוּ
וְלָנוּ אֶת כָּל הַנִּסִּים הָאֵלּוּ. הוֹצִיאָנוּ מֵעַבְדוּת לְחֵרוּת, מִיָּגוֹן
לְשִׂמְחָה, מֵאֵבֶל לְיוֹם טוֹב, וּמֵאֲפֵלָה לְאוֹר גָּדוֹל, וּמִשִּׁעְבּוּד
לִגְאֻלָּה. וְנֹאמַר לְפָנָיו שִׁירָה חֲדָשָׁה; הַלְלוּיָהּ.

לפיכך אנחנו חיבים להודות
להלל שבח לפאר לרומם להדר
לברך לעלה ולקלס למי שעשה
לאבותינו ולנו את כל הנסים האלו.
הוציאנו מעבדות לחרות. מיגון לשמחה
ומאבל ליום טוב. ומאפלה לאור
גדול. ומשעבוד לגאלה. ונאמר
לפניו שירה חדשה
הללויה

Hallelujah!

Praise, you servants of the Lord,
  Praise the name of the Lord.
Blessed be the name of the Lord,
  From this time forth and forever.
From the rising of the sun to where it sets,
  The Lord's name is to be praised.
The Lord is high above all nations,
  His glory is above the heavens.
Who is like to the Lord our God
  That is enthroned on high,
That looks down low
  Upon heaven and upon earth.
He raises up the poor out of the dust,
  And lifts up the needy out of the filth,
That He may set him with princes,
  Even with the princes of His people.
He makes the childless woman into a joyful mother.

Hallelujah!
When Israel went out of Egypt,
  The house of Jacob from an alien people,
Judah became his sanctuary,
  Israel his dominion.
The sea saw it and fled;
  The Jordan turned upstream.
The mountains skipped like rams,
  The hills like young sheep.
What ails you, O sea, that you flee?
  You Jordan, that you turn upstream?
You mountains, that you skip like rams;
  You hills like young sheep?
Tremble, O earth, at the presence of the Lord,
  At the presence of the God of Jacob;
Who turned the rock into a pool of water,
  The flint into a fountain of water.

הללויה

הַלְלוּיָהּ. הַלְלוּ, עַבְדֵי יְיָ, הַלְלוּ אֶת שֵׁם יְיָ. יְהִי שֵׁם יְיָ מְבֹרָךְ, מֵעַתָּה וְעַד עוֹלָם. מִמִּזְרַח שֶׁמֶשׁ עַד מְבוֹאוֹ, מְהֻלָּל שֵׁם יְיָ. רָם עַל כָּל גּוֹיִם יְיָ, עַל הַשָּׁמַיִם כְּבוֹדוֹ. מִי כַּיְיָ אֱלֹהֵינוּ, הַמַּגְבִּיהִי לָשָׁבֶת. הַמַּשְׁפִּילִי לִרְאוֹת בַּשָּׁמַיִם וּבָאָרֶץ. מְקִימִי מֵעָפָר דָּל, מֵאַשְׁפֹּת יָרִים אֶבְיוֹן. לְהוֹשִׁיבִי עִם נְדִיבִים, עִם נְדִיבֵי עַמּוֹ. מוֹשִׁיבִי עֲקֶרֶת הַבַּיִת, אֵם הַבָּנִים שְׂמֵחָה; הַלְלוּיָהּ.

בְּצֵאת יִשְׂרָאֵל מִמִּצְרָיִם, בֵּית יַעֲקֹב מֵעַם לֹעֵז. הָיְתָה יְהוּדָה לְקָדְשׁוֹ, יִשְׂרָאֵל מַמְשְׁלוֹתָיו. הַיָּם רָאָה וַיָּנֹס; הַיַּרְדֵּן יִסֹּב לְאָחוֹר. הֶהָרִים רָקְדוּ כְאֵילִים, גְּבָעוֹת כִּבְנֵי צֹאן. מַה לְּךָ הַיָּם כִּי תָנוּס; הַיַּרְדֵּן, תִּסֹּב לְאָחוֹר. הֶהָרִים, תִּרְקְדוּ כְאֵילִים; גְּבָעוֹת, כִּבְנֵי צֹאן. מִלִּפְנֵי אָדוֹן חוּלִי אָרֶץ, מִלִּפְנֵי אֱלוֹהַּ יַעֲקֹב. הַהֹפְכִי הַצּוּר אֲגַם מָיִם, חַלָּמִישׁ לְמַעְיְנוֹ־מָיִם.

Raise the cup of wine and recite:

Blessed art Thou, O Lord our God, King of the universe, who redeemed our ancestors and us from Egypt, and has enabled us to observe this night, to eat unleavened bread and bitter herbs. May the Lord our God, and the God of our fathers grant us to live to celebrate other festivals and holy seasons. May we rejoice in the building of Thy city, and be gladdened there in Thy service; that we may eat of the sacrifices and of the paschal lambs, whose blood shall be sprinkled on the sides of Thy altar to render them acceptable; then we will chant to Thee a new song for our redemption and for the redemption of our souls. Blessed art Thou, O Lord our God, who redeemed Israel.

בָּרוּךְ אַתָּה, יְיָ אֱלֹהֵינוּ, מֶלֶךְ הָעוֹלָם, אֲשֶׁר גְּאָלָנוּ וְגָאַל אֶת אֲבוֹתֵינוּ מִמִּצְרָיִם, וְהִגִּיעָנוּ לַלַּיְלָה הַזֶּה, לֶאֱכָל־בּוֹ מַצָּה וּמָרוֹר. כֵּן, יְיָ אֱלֹהֵינוּ וֵאלֹהֵי אֲבוֹתֵינוּ, הַגִּיעֵנוּ לְמוֹעֲדִים וְלִרְגָלִים אֲחֵרִים, הַבָּאִים לִקְרָאתֵנוּ לְשָׁלוֹם, שְׂמֵחִים בְּבִנְיַן עִירֶךָ, וְשָׂשִׂים בַּעֲבוֹדָתֶךָ. וְנֹאכַל שָׁם מִן הַזְּבָחִים וּמִן הַפְּסָחִים, אֲשֶׁר יַגִּיעַ דָּמָם עַל קִיר מִזְבַּחֲךָ לְרָצוֹן, וְנוֹדֶה לְךָ שִׁיר חָדָשׁ עַל גְּאֻלָּתֵנוּ וְעַל פְּדוּת נַפְשֵׁנוּ. בָּרוּךְ אַתָּה, יְיָ, גָּאַל יִשְׂרָאֵל.

Blessed art Thou, O Lord our God, King of the universe, Creator of the fruit of the vine.

בָּרוּךְ אַתָּה, יְיָ אֱלֹהֵינוּ, מֶלֶךְ הָעוֹלָם, בּוֹרֵא פְּרִי הַגָּפֶן.

Drink now the second cup of wine.

RAHATZ

Wash the hands pronouncing the benediction:

Blessed be the Lord our God, who has sanctified us with His commandments, and has commanded us to observe washing the hands.

בָּרוּךְ אַתָּה, יְיָ אֱלֹהֵינוּ, מֶלֶךְ הָעוֹלָם, אֲשֶׁר קִדְּשָׁנוּ בְּמִצְוֹתָיו
וְצִוָּנוּ עַל נְטִילַת יָדָיִם.

מוציא מצה

MOTZI, MATZAH

The upper matzah and the portion of the middle matzah is distributed among those present, each one pronouncing the following two benedictions before partaking of the matzah:

Blessed be the Lord our God, King of the universe, who brings forth bread from the earth.

Blessed be the Lord our God, King of the universe, who sanctified us with His commandments, and has commanded us to eat unleavened bread.

בָּרוּךְ אַתָּה, יְיָ אֱלֹהֵינוּ, מֶלֶךְ הָעוֹלָם, הַמּוֹצִיא לֶחֶם מִן
הָאָרֶץ.

בָּרוּךְ אַתָּה, יְיָ אֱלֹהֵינוּ, מֶלֶךְ הָעוֹלָם, אֲשֶׁר קִדְּשָׁנוּ בְּמִצְוֹתָיו
וְצִוָּנוּ עַל אֲכִילַת מַצָּה.

MAROR

Each person receives some bitter herbs dipped in haroseth, and before partaking of same says the following benediction:

Blessed be the Lord of our God, King of the universe, who sanctified us with His commandments, and has commanded us to observe eating bitter herbs.

בָּרוּךְ אַתָּה, יְיָ אֱלֹהֵינוּ, מֶלֶךְ הָעוֹלָם, אֲשֶׁר קִדְּשָׁנוּ בְּמִצְוֹתָיו
וְצִוָּנוּ עַל אֲכִילַת מָרוֹר.

KOREKH

All present now place some of the bitter herbs between two pieces of the lower whole matzah, and they recite:

Thus was Hillel accustomed to do at the time the Temple still stood: He combined unleavened bread and bitter herbs and ate them together, in order to comply with the instruction: "With unleavened bread and bitter herbs, they shall eat the Passover sacrifice."

זֵכֶר לְמִקְדָּשׁ כְּהִלֵּל. כֵּן עָשָׂה הִלֵּל בִּזְמַן שֶׁבֵּית הַמִּקְדָּשׁ הָיָה קַיָּם: הָיָה כּוֹרֵךְ מַצָּה וּמָרוֹר וְאוֹכֵל בְּיַחַד, לְקַיֵּם מַה שֶּׁנֶּאֱמַר: עַל מַצּוֹת וּמְרֹרִים יֹאכְלֻהוּ.

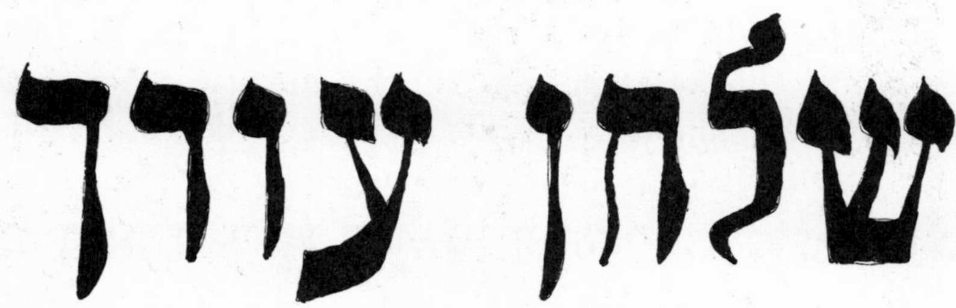

SHULHAN OREKH

Supper is now served.

TZAFOON

At the conclusion of the meal, the leader takes half of the middle matzah which he hid, and gives every one a piece of it.

Gilded domes of
Our Saviour's
Cathedral
in Moscow

BAREKH

The cups are filled with wine, and grace after meals is said.

A Song of Ascents.
When the Lord brings about the return to Zion,
We will be like dreamers!
Our mouth filled with laughter, and our tongue full of song.
Then they will say among the nations:
"The Lord has done great things for them."
The Lord has done great things for us;
We shall rejoice.
End our captivity, O Lord, as the streams in the dry land.
They that sow in tears shall reap in joy.
Though he, that bears the measure of seed, goes out weeping,
He shall come home with joy, bearing his sheaves.

When three or more male persons, over thirteen years of age, have eaten together, one of them is selected to lead the grace, and he says:

Gentlemen, let us say grace.

The company responds:

Blessed be the name of the Lord from henceforth and for ever.

The above verse is repeated by the leader, and then he adds:

With the permission of the respected company, we will bless Him (and if there be ten or more males present, substitute our God for Him), of whose food we have eaten, and through whose goodness we live.

The company responds:

Blessed be He of whose food we have eaten, and through whose goodness we live.

The above verse is repeated by the leader, and the company says grace.
If less than three males above the age of thirteen be present, begin here:

Blessed be He, and blessed be His name.

Blessed be the Lord our God, King of the universe, who sustains the whole world with goodness, with grace, with kindness, and with mercy; He gives food to every creature, for His mercy endures for ever. Through His great goodness, food has never failed us; may it never fail us at any time, for the sake of His great name. He is the God that nourishes, sustains, and deals graciously with every one, and He provides food for all the creatures that He has created. Blessed be the Lord, who gives food to everyone.

ברך

שִׁיר הַמַּעֲלוֹת. בְּשׁוּב יְיָ אֶת שִׁיבַת צִיּוֹן הָיִינוּ כְּחֹלְמִים. אָז יִמָּלֵא שְׂחוֹק פִּינוּ, וּלְשׁוֹנֵנוּ רִנָּה; אָז יֹאמְרוּ בַגּוֹיִם, הִגְדִּיל יְיָ לַעֲשׂוֹת עִם אֵלֶּה. הִגְדִּיל יְיָ לַעֲשׂוֹת עִמָּנוּ, הָיִינוּ שְׂמֵחִים. שׁוּבָה יְיָ אֶת שְׁבִיתֵנוּ, כַּאֲפִיקִים בַּנֶּגֶב. הַזֹּרְעִים בְּדִמְעָה, בְּרִנָּה יִקְצֹרוּ. הָלֹךְ יֵלֵךְ וּבָכֹה נֹשֵׂא מֶשֶׁךְ הַזָּרַע; בֹּא יָבֹא בְרִנָּה נֹשֵׂא אֲלֻמֹּתָיו.

בִּרְכַּת הַמָּזוֹן

רַבּוֹתַי, נְבָרֵךְ.

יְהִי שֵׁם יְיָ מְבֹרָךְ מֵעַתָּה וְעַד עוֹלָם.

בִּרְשׁוּת מָרָנָן וְרַבּוֹתַי נְבָרֵךְ (אֱלֹהֵינוּ) שֶׁאָכַלְנוּ מִשֶּׁלּוֹ.

בָּרוּךְ (אֱלֹהֵינוּ) שֶׁאָכַלְנוּ מִשֶּׁלּוֹ וּבְטוּבוֹ חָיִינוּ.

בָּרוּךְ הוּא וּבָרוּךְ שְׁמוֹ.

בָּרוּךְ אַתָּה, יְיָ אֱלֹהֵינוּ, מֶלֶךְ הָעוֹלָם, הַזָּן אֶת הָעוֹלָם כֻּלּוֹ בְּטוּבוֹ, בְּחֵן בְּחֶסֶד וּבְרַחֲמִים. הוּא נוֹתֵן לֶחֶם לְכָל בָּשָׂר, כִּי לְעוֹלָם חַסְדּוֹ. וּבְטוּבוֹ הַגָּדוֹל תָּמִיד לֹא חָסַר לָנוּ, וְאַל יֶחְסַר לָנוּ מָזוֹן לְעוֹלָם וָעֶד בַּעֲבוּר שְׁמוֹ הַגָּדוֹל. כִּי הוּא אֵל זָן וּמְפַרְנֵס לַכֹּל, וּמֵטִיב לַכֹּל, וּמֵכִין מָזוֹן לְכָל בְּרִיּוֹתָיו אֲשֶׁר בָּרָא. בָּרוּךְ אַתָּה, יְיָ, הַזָּן אֶת הַכֹּל.

We thank Thee, O Lord our God, for having caused our fathers to possess that desirable, good and spacious land; for having brought us forth from the land of Egypt; for having redeemed us from the house of bondage; for Thy covenant sealed in our flesh, for the law which Thou has taught us; for the statutes which Thou hast made known to us; for the life, kindness and mercy which Thou hast graciously bestowed upon us; and for the food which Thou dost nourish and sustain us, every day, every time, and every hour.

For all these things, O Lord our God, we thank Thee and praise Thee; blessed be Thy name forever, by every living creature, forever and ever; as it is written: "When you have eaten and are satisfied, then you shall bless the Lord your God for the good land which He has given you." Blessed art Thou, O Lord, for the Holy Land and for the food.

O Lord our God, have mercy upon Thy people Israel, on Jerusalem Thy city, on Zion the dwelling place of Thy glory, on the house of David your anointed, and on the great holy Temple which was given Thy name. O our God, our Father, be our Shepherd, nourish us, sustain us, support us and relieve us. O Lord our God, relieve us speedily from all our troubles. Let us not, O Lord our God, become dependent upon the gifts of men nor upon their loans, but let us rather depend upon upon Thy full, open, holy and ample hand, that we may never be put to shame or humiliation.

On Sabbath, the following paragraph is added:

May it please Thee O Lord our God, to give us strength to obey Thy commandments, and especially the commandment relating to the seventh day, this great and holy Sabbath. This day is great and holy in Thy sight, to rest and repose thereon, in love, according to the precept of Thy will. May it be Thy will, O Lord our God, that no trouble, no sorrow, and no grief affect us on our day of rest. And let us, O Lord our God, witness the consolation of Zion Thy city, and the rebuilding of Jerusalem Thy holy city, for Thou art the Lord of salvation and of consolation.

נוֹדֶה לְּךָ, יְיָ אֱלֹהֵינוּ, עַל שֶׁהִנְחַלְתָּ לַאֲבוֹתֵינוּ אֶרֶץ חֶמְדָּה טוֹבָה וּרְחָבָה; וְעַל שֶׁהוֹצֵאתָנוּ, יְיָ אֱלֹהֵינוּ, מֵאֶרֶץ מִצְרַיִם, וּפְדִיתָנוּ מִבֵּית עֲבָדִים; וְעַל בְּרִיתְךָ שֶׁחָתַמְתָּ בִּבְשָׂרֵנוּ; וְעַל תּוֹרָתְךָ שֶׁלִּמַּדְתָּנוּ; וְעַל חֻקֶּיךָ שֶׁהוֹדַעְתָּנוּ; וְעַל חַיִּים, חֵן וָחֶסֶד שֶׁחוֹנַנְתָּנוּ; וְעַל אֲכִילַת מָזוֹן שָׁאַתָּה זָן וּמְפַרְנֵס אוֹתָנוּ תָּמִיד, בְּכָל יוֹם וּבְכָל עֵת וּבְכָל שָׁעָה.

וְעַל הַכֹּל, יְיָ אֱלֹהֵינוּ, אֲנַחְנוּ מוֹדִים לָךְ, וּמְבָרְכִים אוֹתָךְ; יִתְבָּרַךְ שִׁמְךָ בְּפִי כָּל חַי תָּמִיד לְעוֹלָם וָעֶד, כַּכָּתוּב: וְאָכַלְתָּ וְשָׂבָעְתָּ, וּבֵרַכְתָּ אֶת יְיָ אֱלֹהֶיךָ עַל הָאָרֶץ הַטֹּבָה אֲשֶׁר נָתַן לָךְ. בָּרוּךְ אַתָּה, יְיָ, עַל הָאָרֶץ וְעַל הַמָּזוֹן.

רַחֵם, יְיָ אֱלֹהֵינוּ, עַל יִשְׂרָאֵל עַמֶּךָ, וְעַל יְרוּשָׁלַיִם עִירֶךָ, וְעַל צִיּוֹן מִשְׁכַּן כְּבוֹדֶךָ, וְעַל מַלְכוּת בֵּית דָּוִד מְשִׁיחֶךָ, וְעַל הַבַּיִת הַגָּדוֹל וְהַקָּדוֹשׁ שֶׁנִּקְרָא שִׁמְךָ עָלָיו. אֱלֹהֵינוּ אָבִינוּ, רְעֵנוּ זוּנֵנוּ, פַּרְנְסֵנוּ וְכַלְכְּלֵנוּ וְהַרְוִיחֵנוּ; וְהַרְוַח לָנוּ, יְיָ אֱלֹהֵינוּ, מְהֵרָה מִכָּל צָרוֹתֵינוּ. וְנָא, אַל תַּצְרִיכֵנוּ, יְיָ אֱלֹהֵינוּ, לֹא לִידֵי מַתְּנַת בָּשָׂר וָדָם וְלֹא לִידֵי הַלְוָאָתָם, כִּי אִם לְיָדְךָ הַמְּלֵאָה הַפְּתוּחָה, הַקְּדוֹשָׁה וְהָרְחָבָה, שֶׁלֹּא נֵבוֹשׁ וְלֹא נִכָּלֵם לְעוֹלָם וָעֶד.

(רְצֵה וְהַחֲלִיצֵנוּ, יְיָ אֱלֹהֵינוּ, בְּמִצְוֹתֶיךָ וּבְמִצְוַת יוֹם הַשְּׁבִיעִי, הַשַּׁבָּת הַגָּדוֹל וְהַקָּדוֹשׁ הַזֶּה; כִּי יוֹם זֶה גָּדוֹל וְקָדוֹשׁ הוּא לְפָנֶיךָ, לִשְׁבָּת־בּוֹ וְלָנוּחַ בּוֹ בְּאַהֲבָה כְּמִצְוַת רְצוֹנֶךָ. וּבִרְצוֹנְךָ הָנַח לָנוּ, יְיָ אֱלֹהֵינוּ, שֶׁלֹּא תְהֵא צָרָה, וְיָגוֹן וַאֲנָחָה, בְּיוֹם מְנוּחָתֵנוּ. וְהַרְאֵנוּ, יְיָ אֱלֹהֵינוּ, בְּנֶחָמַת צִיּוֹן עִירֶךָ, וּבְבִנְיַן יְרוּשָׁלַיִם עִיר קָדְשֶׁךָ, כִּי אַתָּה הוּא בַּעַל הַיְשׁוּעוֹת וּבַעַל הַנֶּחָמוֹת.)

Our God and the God of our fathers! May our remembrance, the remembrance of our fathers, the remembrance of the Messiah, the son of David, Thy servant, the remembrance of Jerusalem, Thy holy city, and the remembrance of all Thy people, the house of Israel, ascend, come, reach, be seen, be accepted, be heard, be thought of, and be remembered before Thee, bringing us deliverance, favor, grace, mercy, life and peace, on this day of the Feast of Unleavened Bread. O Lord our God, remember us this day in kindness, visit us with a blessing, and preserve us for life. With Thy word of salvation and mercy, have pity on us and be gracious to us, for our eyes are ever turned to Thee; for Thou, our Lord, art a gracious and merciful King.

O, rebuild Jerusalem, the Holy City, speedily in our days. Blessed be the Lord our God, who in His mercy will rebuild Jerusalem; Amen.

Blessed be the Lord our God, King of the universe. God is our Father, our mighty Sovereign, our Creator, our Redeemer, our Maker, our Holy One, the Holy One of Jacob, our Shepherd, the Shepherd of Israel; the King who is kind and who deals kindly with everyone; day by day He has dealt kindly with us; He has bestowed, He does bestow, and He will ever bestow upon us grace, favor, loving-kindness, mercy, deliverance, prosperity, blessing, salvation, consolation, sustenance, support, life, peace and all good; may His bounty never fail us.

The All-merciful! May He reign over us for ever.

The All-merciful. May He be praised in heaven and on earth.

The All-merciful! May he be adored throughout all generations, be eternally glorified among us, and be honored among us to all eternity.

The All-merciful! May He sustain us with honor.

The All-merciful! May He break the yoke of the exile from off our necks, and lead us with triumph to our land.

The All-merciful! May He send his ample blessing upon this house and upon this table upon which we ate.

The All-merciful! May He send us Elijah the prophet, of blessed memory, to bring us the good tidings of salvation and consolation.

אֱלֹהֵינוּ וֵאלֹהֵי אֲבוֹתֵינוּ, יַעֲלֶה וְיָבֹא, וְיַגִּיעַ וְיֵרָאֶה, וְיֵרָצֶה וְיִשָּׁמַע, וְיִפָּקֵד וְיִזָּכֵר זִכְרוֹנֵנוּ וּפִקְדוֹנֵנוּ, וְזִכְרוֹן אֲבוֹתֵינוּ, וְזִכְרוֹן מָשִׁיחַ בֶּן דָּוִד עַבְדֶּךָ, וְזִכְרוֹן יְרוּשָׁלַיִם עִיר קָדְשֶׁךָ, וְזִכְרוֹן כָּל עַמְּךָ בֵּית יִשְׂרָאֵל לְפָנֶיךָ, לִפְלֵיטָה וּלְטוֹבָה, לְחֵן וּלְחֶסֶד וּלְרַחֲמִים, לְחַיִּים וּלְשָׁלוֹם, בְּיוֹם חַג הַמַּצּוֹת הַזֶּה. זָכְרֵנוּ, יְיָ אֱלֹהֵינוּ, בּוֹ לְטוֹבָה, וּפָקְדֵנוּ בוֹ לִבְרָכָה, וְהוֹשִׁיעֵנוּ בוֹ לְחַיִּים. וּבִדְבַר יְשׁוּעָה וְרַחֲמִים חוּס וְחָנֵּנוּ, וְרַחֵם עָלֵינוּ וְהוֹשִׁיעֵנוּ כִּי אֵלֶיךָ עֵינֵינוּ, כִּי אֵל מֶלֶךְ חַנּוּן וְרַחוּם אָתָּה.

וּבְנֵה יְרוּשָׁלַיִם עִיר הַקֹּדֶשׁ בִּמְהֵרָה בְיָמֵינוּ. בָּרוּךְ אַתָּה, יְיָ, בּוֹנֵה בְרַחֲמָיו יְרוּשָׁלָיִם, אָמֵן.

בָּרוּךְ אַתָּה, יְיָ אֱלֹהֵינוּ, מֶלֶךְ הָעוֹלָם, הָאֵל, אָבִינוּ, מַלְכֵּנוּ, אַדִּירֵנוּ, בּוֹרְאֵנוּ, גּוֹאֲלֵנוּ, יוֹצְרֵנוּ, קְדוֹשֵׁנוּ, קְדוֹשׁ יַעֲקֹב, רוֹעֵנוּ, רוֹעֵה יִשְׂרָאֵל, הַמֶּלֶךְ הַטּוֹב וְהַמֵּטִיב לַכֹּל, שֶׁבְּכָל יוֹם וָיוֹם הוּא הֵטִיב, הוּא מֵטִיב, הוּא יֵיטִיב לָנוּ. הוּא גְמָלָנוּ, הוּא גוֹמְלֵנוּ, הוּא יִגְמְלֵנוּ לָעַד, לְחֵן וּלְחֶסֶד וּלְרַחֲמִים וּלְרֶוַח, הַצָּלָה וְהַצְלָחָה, בְּרָכָה וִישׁוּעָה, נֶחָמָה פַּרְנָסָה וְכַלְכָּלָה, וְרַחֲמִים וְחַיִּים וְשָׁלוֹם וְכָל טוֹב, וּמִכָּל טוּב לְעוֹלָם אַל יְחַסְּרֵנוּ.

הָרַחֲמָן, הוּא יִמְלוֹךְ עָלֵינוּ לְעוֹלָם וָעֶד.

הָרַחֲמָן, הוּא יִתְבָּרַךְ בַּשָּׁמַיִם וּבָאָרֶץ.

הָרַחֲמָן, הוּא יִשְׁתַּבַּח לְדוֹר דּוֹרִים, וְיִתְפָּאַר בָּנוּ לָעַד וּלְנֵצַח נְצָחִים, וְיִתְהַדַּר בָּנוּ לָעַד וּלְעוֹלְמֵי עוֹלָמִים.

הָרַחֲמָן, הוּא יְפַרְנְסֵנוּ בְּכָבוֹד.

הָרַחֲמָן, הוּא יִשְׁבּוֹר עֻלֵּנוּ מֵעַל צַוָּארֵנוּ, וְהוּא יוֹלִיכֵנוּ קוֹמְמִיּוּת לְאַרְצֵנוּ.

הָרַחֲמָן, הוּא יִשְׁלַח בְּרָכָה מְרֻבָּה בַּבַּיִת הַזֶּה, וְעַל שֻׁלְחָן זֶה שֶׁאָכַלְנוּ עָלָיו.

הָרַחֲמָן, הוּא יִשְׁלַח לָנוּ אֶת אֵלִיָּהוּ הַנָּבִיא, זָכוּר לַטּוֹב, וִיבַשֶּׂר־לָנוּ בְּשׂוֹרוֹת טוֹבוֹת, יְשׁוּעוֹת וְנֶחָמוֹת.

The All-merciful! May He bless my honored father, the master of this house, and my honored mother, the mistress of this house, their household and their children and all that belongs to them; may He bless us and all that belongs to us. As He blessed our ancestors, Abraham, Isaac and Jacob, each one with his unique blessing, thus may He bless us all together with a perfect blessing; and let us say, Amen.

May they in heaven intercede on their behalf and ours, to advocate for enduring peace; and may we receive a blessing from the Lord, and kindness from the God of our salvation. May we find grace and good favor in the sight of God and man.

On Sabbath add the following paragraph:

The All-merciful! May He permit us to inherit the day that is wholly Sabbath and repose in life everlasting.

The All-merciful! May He permit us to inherit the day that is wholly good.
The All-merciful! May He grant us to behold the day of the Messiah, and of the life of the world to come.
A tower of salvation is He to His king; and shows mercy to His anointed, to David and to his seed, for evermore. May He who makes peace in His high heavens, grant peace to us and to all Israel; and let us say: Amen.
O fear the Lord, you, His holy ones; for there is no want to them that fear Him. The young lions may lack, and suffer hunger; but they who seek the Lord lack not any good thing. Give thanks to the Lord, for He is good, for His mercy endures forever. Thou openest Thy hand and satisfiest every living thing with favor. Blessed is the man that trusts in the Lord, and whose trust the Lord is. I have been young, now am old; yet have I not seen the righteous forsaken, nor His seed begging bread. The Lord will give strength to His people; the Lord will bless His people with peace.

Blessed be the Lord our God, King of the universe, who has created the fruit of the vine.

הָרַחֲמָן, הוּא יְבָרֵךְ–אֶת (אָבִי מוֹרִי) בַּעַל הַבַּיִת הַזֶּה וְאֶת (אִמִּי מוֹרָתִי) בַּעֲלַת הַבַּיִת הַזֶּה, אוֹתָם וְאֶת בֵּיתָם וְאֶת זַרְעָם וְאֶת כָּל אֲשֶׁר לָהֶם–אוֹתָנוּ וְאֶת כָּל אֲשֶׁר לָנוּ. כְּמוֹ שֶׁנִּתְבָּרְכוּ אֲבוֹתֵינוּ אַבְרָהָם יִצְחָק וְיַעֲקֹב בַּכֹּל מִכֹּל כֹּל, כֵּן יְבָרֵךְ אוֹתָנוּ, כֻּלָּנוּ יַחַד, בִּבְרָכָה שְׁלֵמָה, וְנֹאמַר אָמֵן.

בַּמָּרוֹם יְלַמְּדוּ (עֲלֵיהֶם וְ)עָלֵינוּ זְכוּת, שֶׁתְּהֵא לְמִשְׁמֶרֶת שָׁלוֹם. וְנִשָּׂא בְרָכָה מֵאֵת יְיָ, וּצְדָקָה מֵאֱלֹהֵי יִשְׁעֵנוּ, וְנִמְצָא חֵן וְשֵׂכֶל טוֹב בְּעֵינֵי אֱלֹהִים וְאָדָם.

(הָרַחֲמָן, הוּא יַנְחִילֵנוּ יוֹם שֶׁכֻּלּוֹ שַׁבָּת וּמְנוּחָה לְחַיֵּי הָעוֹלָמִים.)

הָרַחֲמָן, הוּא יַנְחִילֵנוּ יוֹם שֶׁכֻּלּוֹ טוֹב.

הָרַחֲמָן, הוּא יְזַכֵּנוּ לִימוֹת הַמָּשִׁיחַ וּלְחַיֵּי הָעוֹלָם הַבָּא. מִגְדּוֹל יְשׁוּעוֹת מַלְכּוֹ וְעֹשֶׂה חֶסֶד לִמְשִׁיחוֹ, לְדָוִד וּלְזַרְעוֹ עַד עוֹלָם. עֹשֶׂה שָׁלוֹם בִּמְרוֹמָיו, הוּא יַעֲשֶׂה שָׁלוֹם עָלֵינוּ וְעַל כָּל יִשְׂרָאֵל, וְאִמְרוּ אָמֵן.

יְראוּ אֶת יְיָ קְדֹשָׁיו, כִּי אֵין מַחְסוֹר לִירֵאָיו. כְּפִירִים רָשׁוּ וְרָעֵבוּ, וְדֹרְשֵׁי יְיָ לֹא יַחְסְרוּ כָל טוֹב. הוֹדוּ לַייָ כִּי טוֹב, כִּי לְעוֹלָם חַסְדּוֹ. פּוֹתֵחַ אֶת יָדֶךָ, וּמַשְׂבִּיעַ לְכָל חַי רָצוֹן. בָּרוּךְ הַגֶּבֶר אֲשֶׁר יִבְטַח בַּייָ, וְהָיָה יְיָ מִבְטַחוֹ. נַעַר הָיִיתִי גַּם זָקַנְתִּי, וְלֹא רָאִיתִי צַדִּיק נֶעֱזָב, וְזַרְעוֹ מְבַקֶּשׁ־לָחֶם. יְיָ עֹז לְעַמּוֹ יִתֵּן; יְיָ יְבָרֵךְ אֶת עַמּוֹ בַשָּׁלוֹם.

בָּרוּךְ אַתָּה, יְיָ אֱלֹהֵינוּ, מֶלֶךְ הָעוֹלָם, בּוֹרֵא פְּרִי הַגָּפֶן.

Drink the third cup of wine; then open the door and recite the following:

O pour out Thy wrath upon the nations that know Thee not, and upon the kingdoms that call not upon Thy name. For they have devoured Jacob, and laid waste his land. Pour out Thy indignation upon them, and let the fierceness of Thy anger overtake them. Pursue them in anger, and destroy them from under the heavens of the Lord.

The door is closed.

The fourth cup of wine is now filled.

שְׁפֹךְ חֲמָתְךָ אֶל הַגּוֹיִם אֲשֶׁר לֹא יְדָעוּךָ, וְעַל מַמְלָכוֹת אֲשֶׁר בְּשִׁמְךָ לֹא קָרָאוּ. כִּי אָכַל אֶת יַעֲקֹב, וְאֶת נָוֵהוּ הֵשַׁמּוּ. שְׁפָךְ־עֲלֵיהֶם זַעְמֶךָ, וַחֲרוֹן אַפְּךָ יַשִּׂיגֵם. תִּרְדֹּף בְּאַף וְתַשְׁמִידֵם מִתַּחַת שְׁמֵי יְיָ.

פך
חמתך אל
הגוים
אשר לא
ידעוך ועל
ממלכות
אשר
בשמך לא קראו: כי אכל את
יעקב ואת נוהו השמו: שפך
עליהם זעמך וחרון אפך ישיגם:
תרדוף באף ותשמידם מתחת שמי ייי:

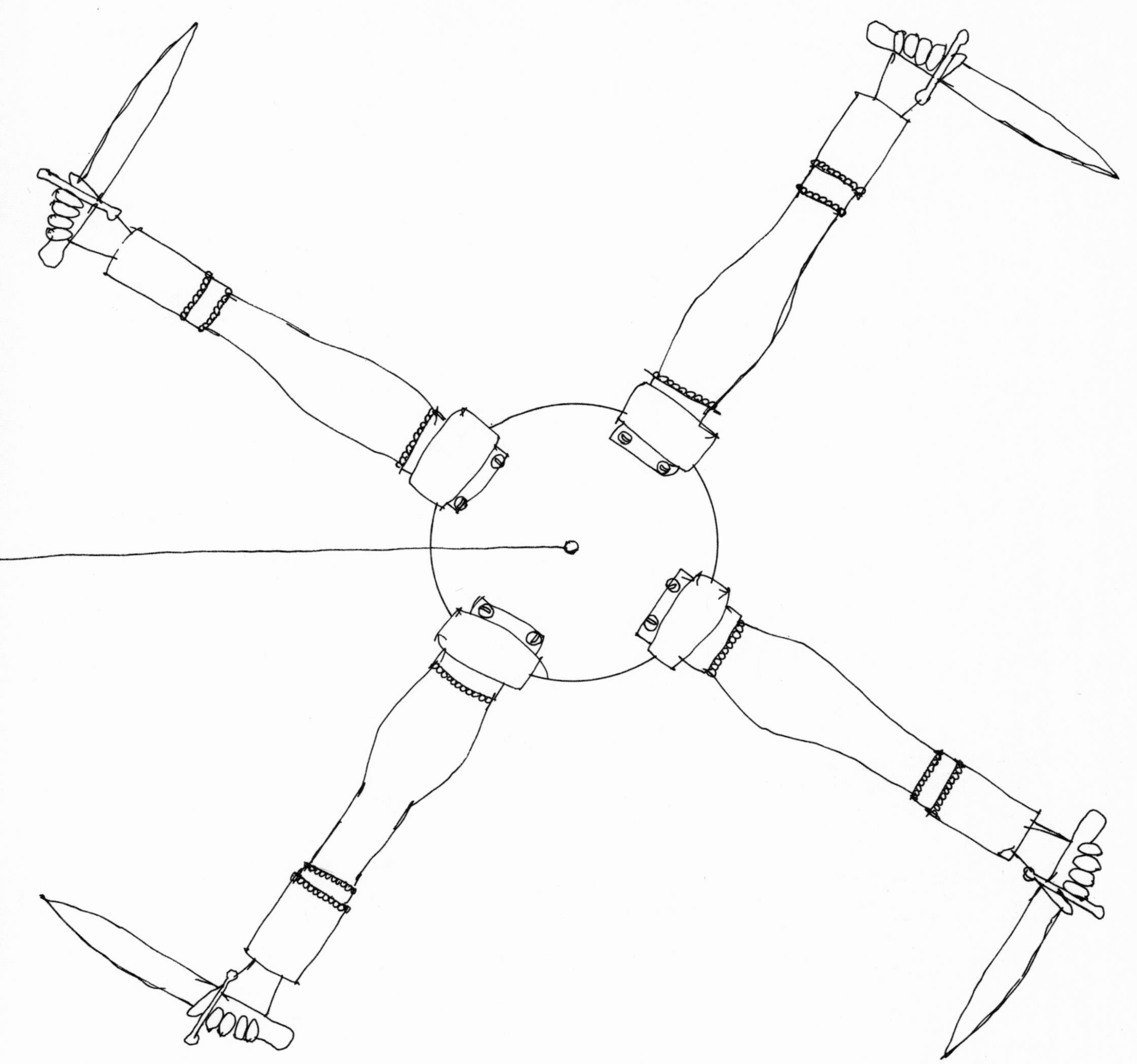

HALLEL

The Hallel Psalms are now recited.

Not to us, O Lord, not to us,
But to Thy name give glory,
For Thy mercy, and for truth's sake.
Should the heathen say:
"Now where is their God?"
But our God is in the heavens;
And He makes what He pleases;
Their idols are silver and gold,
The work of men's hands.
They have mouths, but they cannot speak;
Eyes, but cannot see;
They have ears, but cannot hear;
Noses, but cannot smell;
They have hands, but cannot feel;
Feet, but cannot walk;
Their throats cannot speak;
Those that make them shall be like their idols;
Everyone that trusts in them.
O Israel, trust you in the Lord!
He is their help and their shield!
O house of Aaron, trust you in the Lord!
He is their help and their shield!
You that fear the Lord, trust in the Lord!
He is their help and their shield!

The Lord who has remembered us,
He will bless—
He will bless the house of Israel;
He will bless the house of Aaron;
He will bless those that fear the Lord,
Both small and great.
The Lord increase you more and more,
You and your children.
For you are blest by the Lord,
Who made heaven and earth.
The heavens are the heavens of the Lord;
But the earth He has given to mankind.
The dead do not praise the Lord,
Neither any that go down into silence;
But we will bless the Lord,
From this time forth and forever.
Hallelujah.

I wish the Lord would hear
My voice and my supplications.
Because He has listened to me,
Therefore will I call upon Him all my days.
When the pangs of death are on me,
And the tortures of hell afflict me;
When I find trouble and sorrow.
Then I shall call upon the name of the Lord:
"I beseech Thee, O Lord, deliver my soul."
Gracious is the Lord and righteous;
Our God is compassionate.
The Lord preserves the simple;
I was brought low, and He saved me.
Return, my soul, to Thy rest; For the
Lord has dealt bountifully with you.
For Thou (Lord) hast delivered my soul
from death, Mine eyes from tears,
And my feet from stumbling.
I shall walk before the Lord
In the land of the living.
I trusted even when I spoke:
"I am greatly afflicted."
I said in my haste: "All men are liars."

הלל

לֹא לָנוּ, יְיָ, לֹא לָנוּ, כִּי לְשִׁמְךָ תֵּן כָּבוֹד, עַל חַסְדְּךָ, עַל אֲמִתֶּךָ. לָמָּה יֹאמְרוּ הַגּוֹיִם, אַיֵּה נָא אֱלֹהֵיהֶם. וֵאלֹהֵינוּ בַשָּׁמָיִם; כֹּל אֲשֶׁר חָפֵץ עָשָׂה. עֲצַבֵּיהֶם כֶּסֶף וְזָהָב, מַעֲשֵׂה יְדֵי אָדָם. פֶּה לָהֶם וְלֹא יְדַבֵּרוּ, עֵינַיִם לָהֶם וְלֹא יִרְאוּ. אָזְנַיִם לָהֶם וְלֹא יִשְׁמָעוּ, אַף לָהֶם וְלֹא יְרִיחוּן. יְדֵיהֶם וְלֹא יְמִישׁוּן, רַגְלֵיהֶם וְלֹא יְהַלֵּכוּ; לֹא יֶהְגּוּ בִּגְרוֹנָם. כְּמוֹהֶם יִהְיוּ עֹשֵׂיהֶם, כֹּל אֲשֶׁר בֹּטֵחַ בָּהֶם. יִשְׂרָאֵל, בְּטַח בַּייָ; עֶזְרָם וּמָגִנָּם הוּא. בֵּית אַהֲרֹן, בִּטְחוּ בַייָ; עֶזְרָם וּמָגִנָּם הוּא. יִרְאֵי יְיָ, בִּטְחוּ בַייָ; עֶזְרָם וּמָגִנָּם הוּא.

יְיָ זְכָרָנוּ יְבָרֵךְ; יְבָרֵךְ אֶת בֵּית יִשְׂרָאֵל, יְבָרֵךְ אֶת בֵּית אַהֲרֹן. יְבָרֵךְ יִרְאֵי יְיָ, הַקְּטַנִּים עִם הַגְּדֹלִים. יֹסֵף יְיָ עֲלֵיכֶם, עֲלֵיכֶם וְעַל בְּנֵיכֶם. בְּרוּכִים אַתֶּם לַייָ, עֹשֵׂה שָׁמַיִם וָאָרֶץ. הַשָּׁמַיִם שָׁמַיִם לַייָ, וְהָאָרֶץ נָתַן לִבְנֵי אָדָם. לֹא הַמֵּתִים יְהַלְלוּ יָהּ, וְלֹא כָּל יֹרְדֵי דוּמָה. וַאֲנַחְנוּ נְבָרֵךְ יָהּ מֵעַתָּה וְעַד עוֹלָם; הַלְלוּיָהּ.

אָהַבְתִּי כִּי יִשְׁמַע יְיָ אֶת קוֹלִי תַּחֲנוּנָי. כִּי הִטָּה אָזְנוֹ לִי, וּבְיָמַי אֶקְרָא. אֲפָפוּנִי חֶבְלֵי מָוֶת, וּמְצָרֵי שְׁאוֹל מְצָאוּנִי; צָרָה וְיָגוֹן אֶמְצָא. וּבְשֵׁם יְיָ אֶקְרָא, אָנָּה יְיָ, מַלְּטָה נַפְשִׁי. חַנּוּן יְיָ וְצַדִּיק, וֵאלֹהֵינוּ מְרַחֵם. שֹׁמֵר פְּתָאִים יְיָ; דַּלֹּתִי וְלִי יְהוֹשִׁיעַ. שׁוּבִי נַפְשִׁי לִמְנוּחָיְכִי, כִּי יְיָ גָּמַל עָלָיְכִי. כִּי חִלַּצְתָּ נַפְשִׁי מִמָּוֶת, אֶת עֵינִי מִן דִּמְעָה, אֶת רַגְלִי מִדֶּחִי. אֶתְהַלֵּךְ לִפְנֵי יְיָ, בְּאַרְצוֹת הַחַיִּים. הֶאֱמַנְתִּי כִּי אֲדַבֵּר, אֲנִי עָנִיתִי מְאֹד. אֲנִי אָמַרְתִּי בְחָפְזִי, כָּל הָאָדָם כֹּזֵב.

How can I repay to the Lord
All his bountiful dealings toward me?
I will lift up the cup of salvation,
And call upon the name of the Lord.
My vows will I pay to the Lord,
Yea, in the presence of all His people.
Precious in the sight of the Lord
Is the death of his saints.
I beseech Thee, O Lord, for I am Thy servant;
I am Thy servant, the son of your handmaid;
Thou hast loosed my bands.
I will offer to Thee the sacrifices of thanksgiving,
And I will call upon the name of the Lord.
I will pay my vows unto the Lord,
Yea, in the presence of all His people;
In the courts of the Lord's house,
In the midst of Jerusalem.
Hallelujah.

O praise the Lord, all nations;
Laud Him all peoples.
For His mercy is great towards us;
And the truth of the Lord endures forever.
Hallelujah.

O give thanks to the Lord, for He is good,
For His mercy endures forever.
So let Israel now say:
"For His mercy endures forever."
So let the house of Aaron now say:
"For His mercy endures forever."
So let those who fear the Lord say:
"For His mercy endures forever."
Out of my distress I called upon the Lord;
He answered me handsomely;
The Lord is for me; I will not fear;
What can man do to me?
The Lord is my helper;
And I shall gaze upon those who hate me.
It is better to take refuge in the Lord
Than to trust in man.
It is better to take refuge in the Lord
Than to trust in princes.
All nations may surround me;
In the name of the Lord I will cut them down.
They encircle me, they surround me;
In the name of the Lord I will cut them down;
They surround me like bees;
They are destroyed like thorns in a fire;
In the name of the Lord I will cut them down;
I was off balance;
But the Lord helped me.
The Lord is my strength and song;
And He is my salvation.
The voice of rejoicing and salvation is in the tents of the righteous;
The right hand of the Lord does valiantly;
The right hand of the Lord is exalted;
The right hand of the Lord does valiantly.
I shall not die, but live,
And declare the works of the Lord.
The Lord has chastised me;
But He has not given me over to death.
Open to me the gates of righteousness;
I will enter into them, I will give thanks to the Lord. This is the gate of the Lord;
The righteous shall enter into it.

מָה אָשִׁיב לַייָ כָּל תַּגְמוּלוֹהִי עָלָי. כּוֹס יְשׁוּעוֹת אֶשָּׂא, וּבְשֵׁם יְיָ אֶקְרָא. נְדָרַי לַייָ אֲשַׁלֵּם, נֶגְדָה־נָּא לְכָל עַמּוֹ. יָקָר בְּעֵינֵי יְיָ הַמָּוְתָה לַחֲסִידָיו. אָנָּה יְיָ, כִּי אֲנִי עַבְדֶּךָ, אֲנִי עַבְדְּךָ בֶּן אֲמָתֶךָ; פִּתַּחְתָּ לְמוֹסֵרָי. לְךָ אֶזְבַּח זֶבַח תּוֹדָה, וּבְשֵׁם יְיָ אֶקְרָא. נְדָרַי לַייָ אֲשַׁלֵּם, נֶגְדָה־נָּא לְכָל עַמּוֹ. בְּחַצְרוֹת בֵּית יְיָ, בְּתוֹכֵכִי יְרוּשָׁלָיִם; הַלְלוּיָהּ.

הַלְלוּ אֶת יְיָ, כָּל גּוֹיִם; שַׁבְּחוּהוּ, כָּל הָאֻמִּים. כִּי גָבַר עָלֵינוּ חַסְדּוֹ, וֶאֱמֶת יְיָ לְעוֹלָם; הַלְלוּיָהּ.

הוֹדוּ לַייָ כִּי טוֹב   כִּי לְעוֹלָם חַסְדּוֹ.
יֹאמַר נָא יִשְׂרָאֵל   כִּי לְעוֹלָם חַסְדּוֹ.
יֹאמְרוּ נָא בֵית אַהֲרֹן   כִּי לְעוֹלָם חַסְדּוֹ.
יֹאמְרוּ נָא יִרְאֵי יְיָ   כִּי לְעוֹלָם חַסְדּוֹ.

מִן הַמֵּצַר קָרָאתִי יָּהּ, עָנָנִי בַמֶּרְחָב יָהּ. יְיָ לִי, לֹא אִירָא; מַה יַּעֲשֶׂה לִי אָדָם. יְיָ לִי בְּעֹזְרָי, וַאֲנִי אֶרְאֶה בְשֹׂנְאָי. טוֹב לַחֲסוֹת בַּייָ מִבְּטֹחַ בָּאָדָם. טוֹב לַחֲסוֹת בַּייָ מִבְּטֹחַ בִּנְדִיבִים. כָּל גּוֹיִם סְבָבוּנִי; בְּשֵׁם יְיָ, כִּי אֲמִילַם. סַבּוּנִי גַם סְבָבוּנִי; בְּשֵׁם יְיָ, כִּי אֲמִילַם. סַבּוּנִי כִדְבֹרִים, דֹּעֲכוּ כְּאֵשׁ קוֹצִים; בְּשֵׁם יְיָ, כִּי אֲמִילַם. דָּחֹה דְחִיתַנִי לִנְפֹּל, וַייָ עֲזָרָנִי. עָזִּי וְזִמְרָת יָהּ, וַיְהִי לִי לִישׁוּעָה. קוֹל רִנָּה וִישׁוּעָה בְּאָהֳלֵי צַדִּיקִים; יְמִין יְיָ עֹשָׂה חָיִל. יְמִין יְיָ רוֹמֵמָה, יְמִין יְיָ עֹשָׂה חָיִל. לֹא אָמוּת כִּי אֶחְיֶה, וַאֲסַפֵּר מַעֲשֵׂי יָהּ. יַסֹּר יִסְּרַנִּי יָּהּ, וְלַמָּוֶת לֹא נְתָנָנִי. פִּתְחוּ לִי שַׁעֲרֵי צֶדֶק; אָבֹא בָם, אוֹדֶה יָהּ. זֶה הַשַּׁעַר לַייָ, צַדִּיקִים יָבֹאוּ בוֹ.

I will give thanks to Thee, for Thou hast answered me,
And hast become my salvation. *(Repeat)*
The stone which the builders rejected
Has become the corner-stone. *(Repeat)*
This is the Lord's doing;
It is marvelous in our eyes. *(Repeat)*
This is the day which the Lord has made;
We will rejoice and be glad in it. *(Repeat)*

We beseech Thee, O Lord, help us!
We beseech Thee, O Lord, help us!
We beseech Thee, O Lord, make us prosper!
We beseech Thee, O Lord, make us prosper!

Blessed be he that comes in the name of the Lord;
We bless Thee out of the house of the Lord. *(Repeat)*
The Lord is God, and has given us light;
Order the festival procession with boughs, even to the
horns of the altar. *(Repeat)*
Thou art my God, and I will give thanks to Thee;
Thou art my God, and I will exalt Thee. *(Repeat)*

O give thanks to the Lord, for He is good,
For His mercy endures forever. *(Repeat)*
O give thanks to the God of Gods,
For His mercy endures forever.
O give thanks to the Lord of lords,
For His mercy endures forever.
To Him who alone does great wonders,
For His mercy endures forever.
To Him that by understanding made the heavens,
For His mercy endures forever.
To Him that spread forth the earth above the waters,
For His mercy endures forever.
To Him that made great lights,
For His mercy endures forever;
The sun to rule by day,
For His mercy endures forever;
The moon and stars to rule by night,
For His mercy endures forever.
To Him that smote Egypt in their first-born,
For His mercy endures forever;
And delivered Israel from among them,
For His mercy endures forever;

אוֹדְךָ כִּי עֲנִיתָנִי, וַתְּהִי לִי לִישׁוּעָה.
אֶבֶן מָאֲסוּ הַבּוֹנִים, הָיְתָה לְרֹאשׁ פִּנָּה.
מֵאֵת יְיָ הָיְתָה זֹּאת; הִיא נִפְלָאת בְּעֵינֵינוּ.
זֶה הַיּוֹם עָשָׂה יְיָ, נָגִילָה וְנִשְׂמְחָה בוֹ.

אָנָּא יְיָ, הוֹשִׁיעָה נָּא.
אָנָּא יְיָ, הוֹשִׁיעָה נָּא.
אָנָּא יְיָ, הַצְלִיחָה נָא.
אָנָּא יְיָ, הַצְלִיחָה נָא.

בָּרוּךְ הַבָּא בְּשֵׁם יְיָ; בֵּרַכְנוּכֶם מִבֵּית יְיָ.
אֵל יְיָ וַיָּאֶר לָנוּ, אִסְרוּ חַג בַּעֲבֹתִים, עַד קַרְנוֹת הַמִּזְבֵּחַ.
אֵלִי אַתָּה וְאוֹדֶךָּ, אֱלֹהַי אֲרוֹמְמֶךָּ.
הוֹדוּ לַייָ כִּי טוֹב, כִּי לְעוֹלָם חַסְדּוֹ.

הוֹדוּ לַייָ כִּי טוֹב	כִּי לְעוֹלָם חַסְדּוֹ.
הוֹדוּ לֵאלֹהֵי הָאֱלֹהִים	כִּי לְעוֹלָם חַסְדּוֹ.
הוֹדוּ לַאֲדֹנֵי הָאֲדֹנִים	כִּי לְעוֹלָם חַסְדּוֹ.
לְעֹשֵׂה נִפְלָאוֹת גְּדֹלוֹת לְבַדּוֹ	כִּי לְעוֹלָם חַסְדּוֹ.
לְעֹשֵׂה הַשָּׁמַיִם בִּתְבוּנָה	כִּי לְעוֹלָם חַסְדּוֹ.
לְרוֹקַע הָאָרֶץ עַל הַמָּיִם	כִּי לְעוֹלָם חַסְדּוֹ.
לְעֹשֵׂה אוֹרִים גְּדֹלִים	כִּי לְעוֹלָם חַסְדּוֹ.
אֶת הַשֶּׁמֶשׁ לְמֶמְשֶׁלֶת בַּיּוֹם	כִּי לְעוֹלָם חַסְדּוֹ.
אֶת הַיָּרֵחַ וְכוֹכָבִים לְמֶמְשְׁלוֹת בַּלָּיְלָה	כִּי לְעוֹלָם חַסְדּוֹ.
לְמַכֵּה מִצְרַיִם בִּבְכוֹרֵיהֶם	כִּי לְעוֹלָם חַסְדּוֹ.
וַיּוֹצֵא יִשְׂרָאֵל מִתּוֹכָם	כִּי לְעוֹלָם חַסְדּוֹ.

With a strong hand, and with an outstretched arm,
For His mercy endures forever.
To Him who divided the Red Sea in sunder,
For His mercy endures forever;
And made Israel pass through the midst of it,
For His mercy endures forever;
But overthrew Pharaoh and his host in the Red Sea,
For His mercy endures forever.
To him that led his people through the wilderness,
For His mercy endures forever.
To Him that smote great kings,
For His mercy endures forever;
And slew mighty kings,
For His mercy endures forever;
Sihon, king of the Amorites,
For His mercy endures forever;
And Og, king of Bashan,
For His mercy endures forever;
And gave their land for a heritage,
For His mercy endures forever;
Even a heritage to Israel His people,
For His mercy endures forever.
Who remembered us in our low estate,
For His mercy endures forever;
And has delivered us from our adversaries,
For His mercy endures forever.
Who gives food to all flesh,
For His mercy endures forever.
O give thanks to the God of heaven,
For His mercy endures forever.

The breath of every living being shall bless Thy name, O Lord our God, and the spirit of all flesh shall continually glorify and exalt the mention of Thee, O our Ruler. From the remotest past to eternity, Thou art our God, and besides Thee we have no King who redeems and saves, sets free and delivers, supports and has mercy in all times of trouble and distress; we have no king but Thee. He is God of the first (created beings) and of the last, the God of all creatures, the Lord of all generations, who is extolled with many praises, and who guides His world with loving kindness and His creatures with tender mercies. The Lord slumbers not, nor sleeps; He arouses the sleepers and awakens the slumberers; He makes the dumb to speak, and makes loose the bound; He supports the falling, and raises up the bowed down.

בְּיָד חֲזָקָה וּבִזְרוֹעַ נְטוּיָה כִּי לְעוֹלָם חַסְדּוֹ.
לְגֹזֵר יַם סוּף לִגְזָרִים כִּי לְעוֹלָם חַסְדּוֹ.
וְהֶעֱבִיר יִשְׂרָאֵל בְּתוֹכוֹ כִּי לְעוֹלָם חַסְדּוֹ.
וְנִעֵר פַּרְעֹה וְחֵילוֹ בְיַם סוּף כִּי לְעוֹלָם חַסְדּוֹ.
לְמוֹלִיךְ עַמּוֹ בַּמִּדְבָּר כִּי לְעוֹלָם חַסְדּוֹ.
לְמַכֵּה מְלָכִים גְּדֹלִים כִּי לְעוֹלָם חַסְדּוֹ.
וַיַּהֲרֹג מְלָכִים אַדִּירִים כִּי לְעוֹלָם חַסְדּוֹ.
לְסִיחוֹן מֶלֶךְ הָאֱמֹרִי כִּי לְעוֹלָם חַסְדּוֹ.
וּלְעוֹג מֶלֶךְ הַבָּשָׁן כִּי לְעוֹלָם חַסְדּוֹ.
וְנָתַן אַרְצָם לְנַחֲלָה כִּי לְעוֹלָם חַסְדּוֹ.
נַחֲלָה לְיִשְׂרָאֵל עַבְדּוֹ כִּי לְעוֹלָם חַסְדּוֹ.
שֶׁבְּשִׁפְלֵנוּ זָכַר לָנוּ כִּי לְעוֹלָם חַסְדּוֹ.
וַיִּפְרְקֵנוּ מִצָּרֵינוּ כִּי לְעוֹלָם חַסְדּוֹ.
נֹתֵן לֶחֶם לְכָל בָּשָׂר כִּי לְעוֹלָם חַסְדּוֹ.
הוֹדוּ לְאֵל הַשָּׁמָיִם כִּי לְעוֹלָם חַסְדּוֹ.

נִשְׁמַת כָּל חַי תְּבָרֵךְ אֶת שִׁמְךָ, יְיָ אֱלֹהֵינוּ, וְרוּחַ כָּל בָּשָׂר תְּפָאֵר וּתְרוֹמֵם זִכְרְךָ, מַלְכֵּנוּ, תָּמִיד. מִן הָעוֹלָם וְעַד הָעוֹלָם אַתָּה אֵל, וּמִבַּלְעָדֶיךָ אֵין לָנוּ מֶלֶךְ גּוֹאֵל וּמוֹשִׁיעַ, פּוֹדֶה וּמַצִּיל וּמְפַרְנֵס, וּמְרַחֵם בְּכָל עֵת צָרָה וְצוּקָה; אֵין לָנוּ מֶלֶךְ אֶלָּא אָתָּה. אֱלֹהֵי הָרִאשׁוֹנִים וְהָאַחֲרוֹנִים, אֱלוֹהַּ כָּל בְּרִיּוֹת, אֲדוֹן כָּל תּוֹלָדוֹת, הַמְהֻלָּל בְּרֹב הַתִּשְׁבָּחוֹת, הַמְנַהֵג עוֹלָמוֹ בְּחֶסֶד וּבְרִיּוֹתָיו בְּרַחֲמִים. וַיְיָ לֹא יָנוּם וְלֹא יִישָׁן, הַמְעוֹרֵר יְשֵׁנִים, וְהַמֵּקִיץ נִרְדָּמִים, וְהַמֵּשִׂיחַ אִלְּמִים, וְהַמַּתִּיר אֲסוּרִים, וְהַסּוֹמֵךְ נוֹפְלִים, וְהַזּוֹקֵף כְּפוּפִים. לְךָ לְבַדְּךָ אֲנַחְנוּ מוֹדִים.

To Thee alone we give thanks. Though our mouths were full of song as the sea, our tongues full of exultation as its numerous waves, and our lips full of praise as the great expanse of the sky, though our eyes shone with light like the sun and the moon, and our hands were spread forth like the eagles of the heaven, and our feet were swift as the hind's, we should still be unable to thank Thee and to bless Thy name, O Lord our God and God of our fathers, for one-thousandth or for one ten-thousandth part of the bounties which Thou hast bestowed upon our fathers and upon us. Thou hast redeemed us from Egypt, O Lord our God, and released us from the house of bondage; during famine fed us, and sustained us in plenty; from the sword rescued us, from pestilence saved us, and from sore, lasting diseases delivered us. Thy tender mercies have helped us, and Thy loving kindness has not left us; forsake us not, O Lord our God, forever. Therefore, the limbs which Thou hast spread forth upon us, and the spirit and breath Thou hast breathed into our nostrils, and the tongue set in our mouths, they shall bend to Thee and whoever is lofty shall bow before Thee; all hearts shall fear Thee, and all inward parts and reins shall sing to Thy name, according to what is written: "All my bones shall say: 'Lord who is like Thee, who delivers the poor from him that is too strong for him, yea, the poor and the needy from him that spoils them.'" Who is like Thee, who is equal to Thee, and who can be compared to Thee, O God, great, mighty and awe-inspiring, most-high God, possesor of heaven and earth? We will praise, laud and glorify Thee, and we will bless Thy holy name, as it is said: "A Psalm of David. Bless the Lord, O my soul; and all that is with me, bless His Holy name."

O God, Thou art powerful in Thy might, great in Thy glorious name, mighty forever, and awe-inspiring by Thy awe-inspiring acts, the King who sits upon a high and lofty throne.

He who inhabits eternity, exalted and holy in His name, and it is written: "Rejoice in the Lord, O you righteous, praise is comely for the upright."

אִלּוּ פִינוּ מָלֵא שִׁירָה כַּיָּם, וּלְשׁוֹנֵנוּ רִנָּה כַּהֲמוֹן גַּלָּיו, וְשִׂפְתוֹתֵינוּ שֶׁבַח כְּמֶרְחֲבֵי רָקִיעַ, וְעֵינֵינוּ מְאִירוֹת כַּשֶּׁמֶשׁ וְכַיָּרֵחַ, וְיָדֵינוּ פְרוּשׂוֹת כְּנִשְׁרֵי שָׁמָיִם, וְרַגְלֵינוּ קַלּוֹת כָּאַיָּלוֹת, אֵין אֲנַחְנוּ מַסְפִּיקִים לְהוֹדוֹת לְךָ, יְיָ אֱלֹהֵינוּ וֵאלֹהֵי אֲבוֹתֵינוּ, וּלְבָרֵךְ אֶת שִׁמְךָ עַל אַחַת מֵאֶלֶף (אֶלֶף) אַלְפֵי אֲלָפִים וְרִבֵּי רְבָבוֹת פְּעָמִים הַטּוֹבוֹת שֶׁעָשִׂיתָ עִם אֲבוֹתֵינוּ וְעִמָּנוּ. מִמִּצְרַיִם גְּאַלְתָּנוּ, יְיָ אֱלֹהֵינוּ, וּמִבֵּית עֲבָדִים פְּדִיתָנוּ; בְּרָעָב זַנְתָּנוּ וּבְשָׂבָע כִּלְכַּלְתָּנוּ; מֵחֶרֶב הִצַּלְתָּנוּ וּמִדֶּבֶר מִלַּטְתָּנוּ, וּמֵחֳלָיִם רָעִים וְנֶאֱמָנִים דִּלִּיתָנוּ. עַד הֵנָּה עֲזָרוּנוּ רַחֲמֶיךָ וְלֹא עֲזָבוּנוּ חֲסָדֶיךָ; וְאַל תִּטְּשֵׁנוּ, יְיָ אֱלֹהֵינוּ, לָנֶצַח. עַל כֵּן, אֵבָרִים שֶׁפִּלַּגְתָּ בָּנוּ, וְרוּחַ וּנְשָׁמָה שֶׁנָּפַחְתָּ בְּאַפֵּינוּ, וְלָשׁוֹן אֲשֶׁר שַׂמְתָּ בְּפִינוּ, הֵן הֵם יוֹדוּ וִיבָרְכוּ, וִישַׁבְּחוּ וִיפָאֲרוּ, וִירוֹמְמוּ וְיַעֲרִיצוּ, וְיַקְדִּישׁוּ וְיַמְלִיכוּ אֶת שִׁמְךָ, מַלְכֵּנוּ. כִּי כָל פֶּה לְךָ יוֹדֶה, וְכָל לָשׁוֹן לְךָ תִשָּׁבַע, וְכָל בֶּרֶךְ לְךָ תִכְרַע, וְכָל קוֹמָה לְפָנֶיךָ תִשְׁתַּחֲוֶה. וְכָל לְבָבוֹת יִירָאוּךָ, וְכָל קֶרֶב וּכְלָיוֹת יְזַמְּרוּ לִשְׁמֶךָ, כַּדָּבָר שֶׁכָּתוּב: כָּל עַצְמוֹתַי תֹּאמַרְנָה, יְיָ מִי כָמוֹךָ, מַצִּיל עָנִי מֵחָזָק מִמֶּנּוּ, וְעָנִי וְאֶבְיוֹן מִגֹּזְלוֹ. מִי יִדְמֶה לָּךְ, וּמִי יִשְׁוֶה לָּךְ, וּמִי יַעֲרָךְ־לָךְ, הָאֵל הַגָּדוֹל, הַגִּבּוֹר וְהַנּוֹרָא, אֵל עֶלְיוֹן, קֹנֵה שָׁמַיִם וָאָרֶץ. נְהַלֶּלְךָ וּנְשַׁבֵּחֲךָ וּנְפָאֶרְךָ, וּנְבָרֵךְ אֶת שֵׁם קָדְשֶׁךָ, כָּאָמוּר: לְדָוִד, בָּרְכִי נַפְשִׁי אֶת יְיָ, וְכָל קְרָבַי אֶת שֵׁם קָדְשׁוֹ.

הָאֵל בְּתַעֲצֻמוֹת עֻזֶּךָ, הַגָּדוֹל בִּכְבוֹד שְׁמֶךָ, הַגִּבּוֹר לָנֶצַח וְהַנּוֹרָא בְּנוֹרְאוֹתֶיךָ, הַמֶּלֶךְ הַיּוֹשֵׁב עַל כִּסֵּא רָם וְנִשָּׂא.

שׁוֹכֵן עַד, מָרוֹם וְקָדוֹשׁ שְׁמוֹ. וְכָתוּב: רַנְּנוּ צַדִּיקִים בַּייָ, לַיְשָׁרִים נָאוָה תְהִלָּה.

By the mouth of the upright Thou shalt be praised, by the words of the righteous Thou shalt be blessed, by the tongue of the loving ones Thou shalt be extolled, and in the midst of the holy Thou shalt be hallowed.

From generation to generation, in the assemblies of tens of thousands of Thy people, the house of Israel, Thy name is glorified with joyous song, O our King. For such is the duty of of all creatures toward Thee, O Lord our God and God of our fathers, to give thanks, to praise, to laud, to glorify, to extol, to honor, to bless, to exalt, and to adore Thee, even surpassing all the words of song and praise of David, the son of Jesse, Thy servant and Thy anointed one.

Praised be Thy name forever, O our God, the great and holy God and King, in heaven and on earth; for to Thee, O Lord our God and God of our fathers, are becoming song and praise, hymn and psalm, strength and dominion, victory greatness and might, renown and glory, holiness and kingship, blessings and thanksgivings from henceforth even forever.

For it is proper to give thanks to Thee, and becoming to sing praises to Thy name, because from the remotest past to eternity Thou art our God. Blessed art Thou, O Lord our God, King extolled with praises.

Blessed art Thou, O Lord our God, King of the universe, who hast created the fruit of the vine.

Drink the fourth cup of wine and the following concluding grace is recited:

Blessed art Thou, O Lord our God, King of the universe, for the vine and the fruit of the vine, for the produce of the soil, for the desirable, good and spacious land which Thou were pleased to give as a heritage to our fathers, that they might eat of its fruit and be satisfied with its goodness. Have mercy, O Lord our God, upon Zion, the abiding place of Thy glory, and upon Thy altar and upon Thy Temple. Rebuild Jerusalem, the Holy City, speedily in our days; lead us there and make us rejoice in its rebuilding; may we eat of the fruit of the land, and be satisfied with its goodness; and we will praise Thee for it in holiness and purity. (On Sabbath, say: Be pleased to fortify us on this Sabbath day, and) make us rejoice on this Feast of Unleavened Bread, for Thou, O Lord, art kind and dealest kindly with every one; and we give Thee thanks for the land and for the fruit of the vine. Blessed art Thou, O Lord, for the land and for the fruit of the vine.

בְּפִי יְשָׁרִים תִּתְהַלָּל,
וּבְדִבְרֵי צַדִּיקִים תִּתְבָּרַךְ,
וּבִלְשׁוֹן חֲסִידִים תִּתְרוֹמָם,
וּבְקֶרֶב קְדוֹשִׁים תִּתְקַדָּשׁ.

וּבְמַקְהֲלוֹת רִבְבוֹת עַמְּךָ בֵּית יִשְׂרָאֵל בְּרִנָּה יִתְפָּאַר שִׁמְךָ, מַלְכֵּנוּ, בְּכָל דּוֹר וָדוֹר; שֶׁכֵּן חוֹבַת כָּל הַיְצוּרִים לְפָנֶיךָ, יְיָ אֱלֹהֵינוּ וֵאלֹהֵי אֲבוֹתֵינוּ, לְהוֹדוֹת, לְהַלֵּל, לְשַׁבֵּחַ, לְפָאֵר, לְרוֹמֵם, לְהַדֵּר, לְבָרֵךְ, לְעַלֵּה וּלְקַלֵּס עַל כָּל דִּבְרֵי שִׁירוֹת וְתִשְׁבְּחוֹת דָּוִד בֶּן־יִשַׁי עַבְדְּךָ מְשִׁיחֶךָ.

יִשְׁתַּבַּח שִׁמְךָ לָעַד, מַלְכֵּנוּ, הָאֵל הַמֶּלֶךְ הַגָּדוֹל וְהַקָּדוֹשׁ, בַּשָּׁמַיִם וּבָאָרֶץ. כִּי לְךָ נָאֶה, יְיָ אֱלֹהֵינוּ וֵאלֹהֵי אֲבוֹתֵינוּ, שִׁיר וּשְׁבָחָה, הַלֵּל וְזִמְרָה, עֹז וּמֶמְשָׁלָה, נֶצַח, גְּדֻלָּה וּגְבוּרָה, תְּהִלָּה וְתִפְאֶרֶת, קְדֻשָּׁה וּמַלְכוּת, בְּרָכוֹת וְהוֹדָאוֹת, מֵעַתָּה וְעַד עוֹלָם. בָּרוּךְ אַתָּה, יְיָ, אֵל מֶלֶךְ גָּדוֹל בַּתִּשְׁבָּחוֹת, אֵל הַהוֹדָאוֹת, אֲדוֹן הַנִּפְלָאוֹת, הַבּוֹחֵר בְּשִׁירֵי זִמְרָה, מֶלֶךְ, אֵל, חֵי הָעוֹלָמִים.

בָּרוּךְ אַתָּה, יְיָ אֱלֹהֵינוּ, מֶלֶךְ הָעוֹלָם, בּוֹרֵא פְּרִי הַגָּפֶן.

בָּרוּךְ אַתָּה, יְיָ אֱלֹהֵינוּ, מֶלֶךְ הָעוֹלָם, עַל הַגֶּפֶן וְעַל פְּרִי הַגֶּפֶן, וְעַל תְּנוּבַת הַשָּׂדֶה, וְעַל אֶרֶץ חֶמְדָּה טוֹבָה וּרְחָבָה שֶׁרָצִיתָ וְהִנְחַלְתָּ לַאֲבוֹתֵינוּ לֶאֱכֹל מִפִּרְיָהּ וְלִשְׂבֹּעַ מִטּוּבָהּ. רַחֶם־נָא, יְיָ אֱלֹהֵינוּ, עַל יִשְׂרָאֵל עַמֶּךָ, וְעַל יְרוּשָׁלַיִם עִירֶךָ, וְעַל צִיּוֹן מִשְׁכַּן כְּבוֹדֶךָ, וְעַל מִזְבְּחֶךָ וְעַל הֵיכָלֶךָ. וּבְנֵה יְרוּשָׁלַיִם עִיר הַקֹּדֶשׁ בִּמְהֵרָה בְיָמֵינוּ, וְהַעֲלֵנוּ לְתוֹכָהּ וְשַׂמְּחֵנוּ בְּבִנְיָנָהּ, וְנֹאכַל מִפִּרְיָהּ וְנִשְׂבַּע מִטּוּבָהּ, וּנְבָרֶכְךָ עָלֶיהָ בִּקְדֻשָּׁה וּבְטָהֳרָה. (רְצֵה וְהַחֲלִיצֵנוּ בְּיוֹם הַשַּׁבָּת הַזֶּה, וְ)שַׂמְּחֵנוּ בְּיוֹם חַג הַמַּצּוֹת הַזֶּה. כִּי אַתָּה, יְיָ, טוֹב וּמֵטִיב לַכֹּל, וְנוֹדֶה לְּךָ עַל הָאָרֶץ וְעַל פְּרִי הַגָּפֶן. בָּרוּךְ אַתָּה, יְיָ, עַל הָאָרֶץ וְעַל פְּרִי הַגָּפֶן.

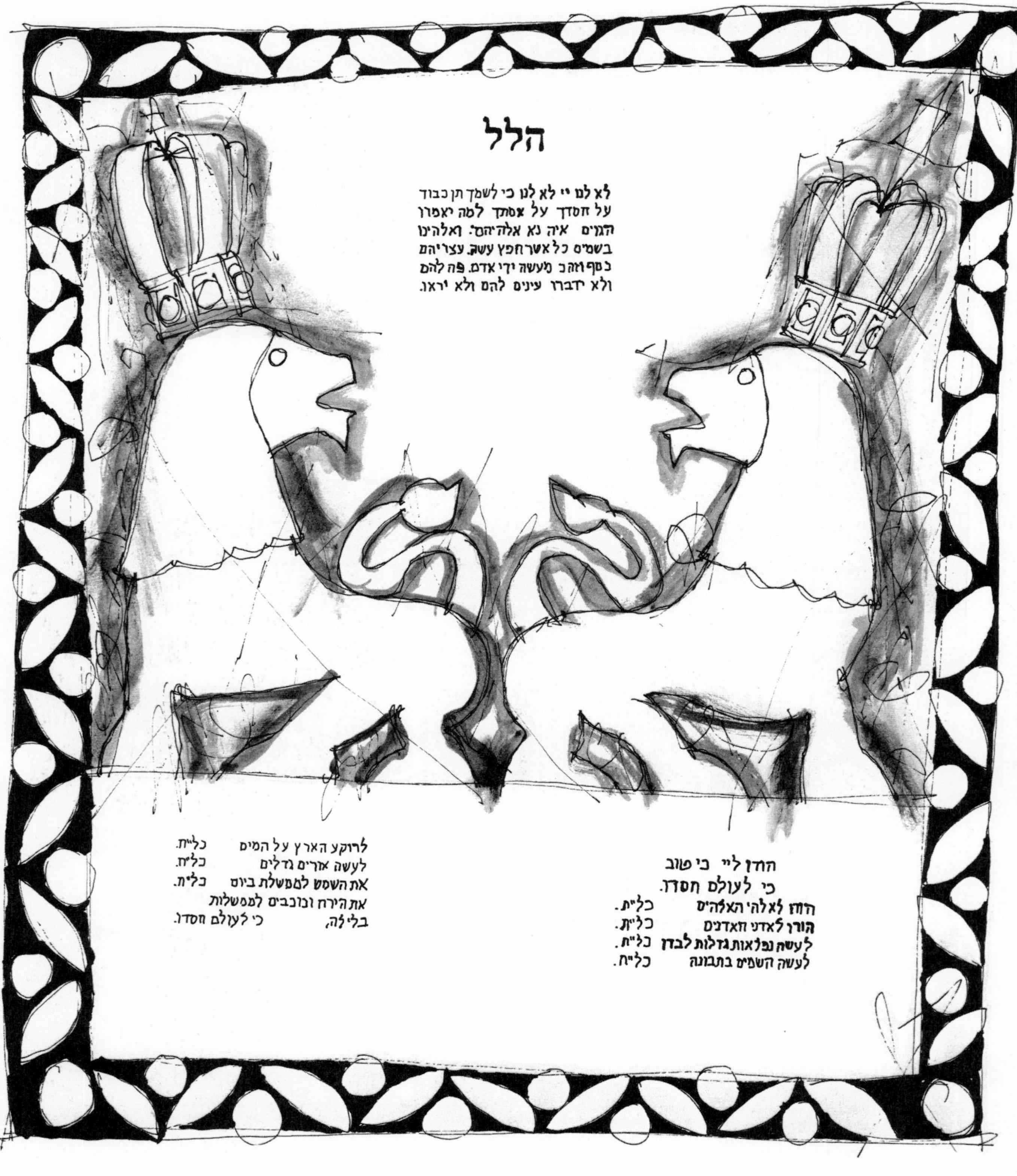

הלל
לא לנו יי לא לנו כי לשמך תן כבוד
על חסדך על אמתך למה יאמרו
הגוים איה נא אלהיהם: ואלהינו
בשמים כל אשר חפץ עשה. עצביהם
כסף וזהב מעשה ידי אדם. פה להם
ולא ידברו עינים להם ולא יראו.
הודו ליי כי טוב
כי לעולם חסדו.
הודו לאלהי האלהים כל״ת.
הודו לאדני האדנים כל״ת.
לעשה נפלאות גדלות לבדו כל״ת.
לעשה השמים בתבונה כל״ח.
לרוקע הארץ על המים כל״ת.
לעשה אורים גדלים כל״ת.
את השמש לממשלת ביום כל״ת.
את הירח וכוכבים לממשלות
בלילה, כי לעולם חסדו.

נרצה

The seder of the Passover is now complete, according to the laws, rules and customs. As we have been privileged to celebrate it this year, may we be worthy to actually offer it in the Holy Land. O Pure One, who abides in the Temple, raise up Thy numberless people. O speedily lead the branches Thou hast planted, as free men to Zion, with songs of rejoicing.

חֲסַל סִדּוּר פֶּסַח כְּהִלְכָתוֹ,
כְּכָל מִשְׁפָּטוֹ וְחֻקָּתוֹ;
כַּאֲשֶׁר זָכִינוּ לְסַדֵּר אוֹתוֹ,
כֵּן נִזְכֶּה לַעֲשׂוֹתוֹ.

זָךְ שׁוֹכֵן מְעוֹנָה,
קוֹמֵם קְהַל עֲדַת מִי מָנָה;
בְּקָרוֹב נַהֵל נִטְעֵי כַנָּה,
פְּדוּיִם לְצִיּוֹן בְּרִנָּה.

Next year in Jerusalem!

לְשָׁנָה הַבָּאָה בִּירוּשָׁלָיִם.

The following is said on the first night of Passover:

AND THUS IT CAME TO PASS AT MIDNIGHT

Thou didst perform many miracles at night:
In the beginning of the first watch of this night,
The righteous Abraham triumphed when he divided
his forces at night.
And it came to pass at midnight.
Thou didst warn the king of Gerar in a dream at night.
Frightened the Aramean (Laban) in the dark of night.
And Israel wrestled with an angel and overcame him at night.
And it came to pass at midnight.
The first-born of the Egyptians were slain at midnight;
Their strength left them when they awoke at night;
The army of the prince of Haroseth (Sisera) thou didst
overthrow with the stars of the night.
And it came to pass at midnight.
The blasphemer (Sennacherib) planned to lift up his hand
against the beloved (Zion).
But Thou covered him with disgrace by slaying many
of his men at night.
The idol Bel (god of the Babylonians) and its pedestal
fell in the dark of night.
To the greatly beloved man (Daniel) was revealed
the vision at night.
And it came to pass at midnight.
He who became intoxicated by drinking from the holy
vessels was killed on that night.
He who was rescued from the den of lions, interpreted the
dreadful dreams of the night.
The Agagite (Haman) wrote hate letters at night.
And it came to pass at midnight.
Thou didst bring victory over him by disturbing the sleep
(of the king) at night.
Thou shall bring destruction for the sake of those who say to
the Watchman: "O what of the night (exile)?"
He cried like a watchman and said: "The morning (freedom)
is come as well as the night."
And it came to pass at midnight.
O draw nigh the day, that is neither day nor night
(day of redemption).
O Most High, make it known that Thine is the day
as well as the night.
Appoint watchmen for your city all day and all night.
O make bright, like the very day, the darkness of the night.
And it came to pass at midnight.

וּבְכֵן, וַיְהִי בַּחֲצִי הַלַּיְלָה.

אָ ז רוֹב נִסִּים הִפְלֵאתָ בַּלַּיְלָה,
בְּ רֹאשׁ אַשְׁמוּרוֹת זֶה הַלַּיְלָה,
גֵּ ר צֶדֶק נִצַּחְתּוֹ כְּנֶחֱלַק לוֹ לַיְלָה.
וַיְהִי בַּחֲצִי הַלַּיְלָה.

דָּ נְתָּ מֶלֶךְ גְּרָר בַּחֲלוֹם הַלַּיְלָה,
הִ פְחַדְתָּ אֲרַמִּי בְּאֶמֶשׁ לַיְלָה,
וַ יָּשַׂר יִשְׂרָאֵל לְמַלְאָךְ וַיּוּכַל לוֹ לַיְלָה.
וַיְהִי בַּחֲצִי הַלַּיְלָה.

זֶ רַע בְּכוֹרֵי פַתְרוֹס מָחַצְתָּ בַּחֲצִי הַלַּיְלָה,
חֵ ילָם לֹא מָצְאוּ בְּקוּמָם בַּלַּיְלָה,
טִ יסַת נְגִיד חֲרֹשֶׁת סִלִּיתָ בְכוֹכְבֵי לַיְלָה.
וַיְהִי בַּחֲצִי הַלַּיְלָה.

יָ עַץ מְחָרֵף לְנוֹפֵף אִוּוּי הוֹבַשְׁתָּ פְגָרָיו בַּלַּיְלָה,
כָּ רַע בֵּל וּמַצָּבוֹ בְּאִישׁוֹן לַיְלָה,
לְ אִישׁ חֲמוּדוֹת נִגְלָה רָז חֲזוֹת לַיְלָה.
וַיְהִי בַּחֲצִי הַלַּיְלָה.

מִ שְׁתַּכֵּר בִּכְלֵי קֹדֶשׁ נֶהֱרַג בּוֹ בַלַּיְלָה,
נ וֹשַׁע מִבּוֹר אֲרָיוֹת פּוֹתֵר בִּעֲתוּתֵי לַיְלָה,
שִׂ נְאָה נָטַר אֲגָגִי וְכָתַב סְפָרִים בַּלַּיְלָה.
וַיְהִי בַּחֲצִי הַלַּיְלָה.

ע וֹרַרְתָּ נִצְחֲךָ עָלָיו בְּנֶדֶד שְׁנַת לַיְלָה,
פּ וּרָה תִדְרוֹךְ לְשׁוֹמֵר מַה מִּלַּיְלָה,
צָ רַח כַּשּׁוֹמֵר וְשָׂח אָתָא בֹקֶר וְגַם לַיְלָה.
וַיְהִי בַּחֲצִי הַלַּיְלָה.

קָ רֵב יוֹם אֲשֶׁר הוּא לֹא יוֹם וְלֹא לַיְלָה,
רָ ם הוֹדַע כִּי לְךָ הַיּוֹם אַף לְךָ הַלַּיְלָה,
שׁ וֹמְרִים הַפְקֵד לְעִירְךָ כָּל הַיּוֹם וְכָל הַלַּיְלָה,
תָּ אִיר כְּאוֹר יוֹם חֶשְׁכַת לַיְלָה.
וַיְהִי בַּחֲצִי הַלַּיְלָה.

AND THUS IT CAME TO PASS AT MIDNIGHT

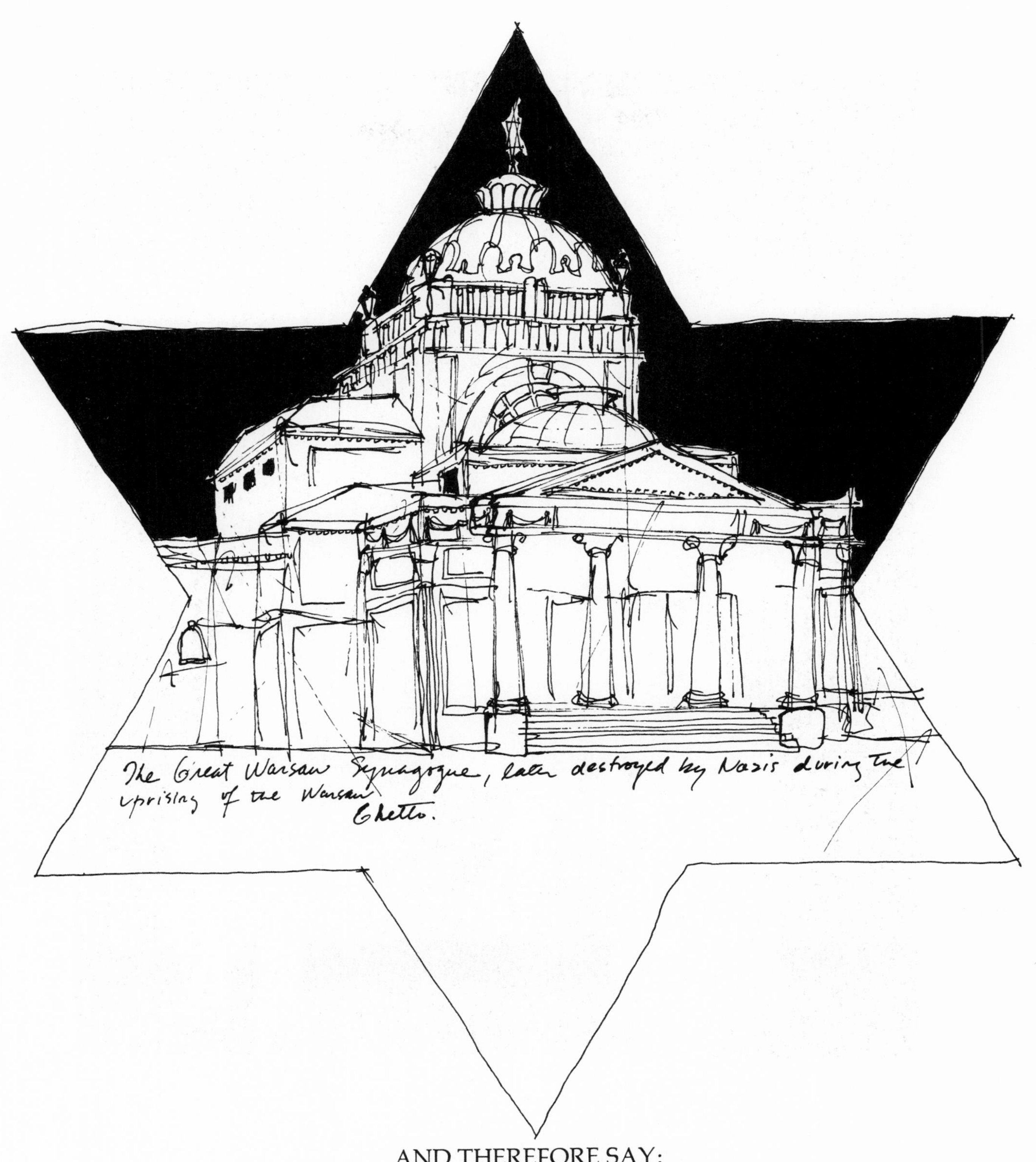

The Great Warsaw Synagogue, later destroyed by Nazis during the uprising of the Warsaw Ghetto.

AND THEREFORE SAY:
"THIS IS THE SACRIFICE OF THE PASSOVER."

The second hymn recounts the events which, according to legend, took place (or are to take place) at the time of Passover. In our own century, the Warsaw Ghetto uprising coincided with the Passover.

The following is said on the Second Night of Passover:

AND THEREFORE SAY:
"THIS IS THE SACRIFICE OF THE PASSOVER."

The might of Thy power was wonderfully shown on the Passover.
At the head of all solemn festivals didst Thou raise the Passover.
Thou didst reveal our destiny to Abraham at midnight of Passover.
And you shall say: "This is the Passover sacrifice."
Thou didst knock at his door at the noon of Passover.
He provided the angels with unleavened cake on Passover.
"And he ran to the herd," predicting the offering of the Passover.
And you shall say: "This is the Passover sacrifice."
The Sodomites drew upon themselves the anger of God,
and were consumed by fire on the Passover.
Lot was rescued from the wicked, and he baked unleavened
bread for the Passover.
Thou didst sweep away the land of Moph and Noph (Egypt)
when Thou didst pass through on the Passover.
And you shall say: "This is the Passover sacrifice."
O Lord! the head of every first born Thou didst crush on
this watchful night of Passover.
O Almighty! yet Thou didst pass over Thy first-born son (Israel)
because of the blood-mark of the Passover;
Thou didst not permit the destroyer to enter my doors on Passover.
And you shall say: "This is the Passover sacrifice."
The strongly fortified city (Jericho) fell in the season of Passover.
Midian was destroyed by (the dream of) the barley-cake,
the Omer offering brought on the Passover.
The mighty warriors of Pul and Lud (Assyria) were consumed
with burning heat on the Passover.
And you shall say: "This is the Passover sacrifice."
(Said Sennacherib): "This day we shall halt yet at Nob,"
before the advent of the Passover.
Thy hand wrote on the wall the doom of Babylon on the Passover.
When the lamps were lit, and the tables were set on Passover.
And you shall say: "This is the Passover sacrifice."
Esther assembled the congregation for a three days' fast
on the Passover.
The chief of the wicked tribe (Haman) was executed on a
gallows of fifty cubits, on the Passover.
A double punishment Thou shalt bring in a moment on Utz
on the Passover.
And you shall say: "This is the Passover sacrifice."

וּבְכֵן, וַאֲמַרְתֶּם זֶבַח פֶּסַח.

אֹ מֶץ גְּבוּרוֹתֶיךָ הִפְלֵאתָ בַּפֶּסַח,
בְּ רֹאשׁ כָּל מוֹעֲדוֹת נִשֵּׂאתָ פֶּסַח,
גִּ לִּיתָ לְאֶזְרָחִי חֲצוֹת לֵיל פֶּסַח. וַאֲמַרְתֶּם זֶבַח פֶּסַח.

דְּ לָתָיו דָּפַקְתָּ כְּחֹם הַיּוֹם בַּפֶּסַח,
הִ סְעִיד נוֹצְצִים עֻגוֹת מַצּוֹת בַּפֶּסַח,
וְ אֶל הַבָּקָר רָץ זֵכֶר לְשׁוֹר עֵרֶךְ פֶּסַח. וַאֲמַרְתֶּם זֶבַח פֶּסַח.

זֹ עֲמוּ סְדוֹמִים וְלֹהֲטוּ בָּאֵשׁ בַּפֶּסַח,
חֻ לַּץ לוֹט מֵהֶם וּמַצּוֹת אָפָה בְּקֵץ פֶּסַח,
טִ אטֵאתָ אַדְמַת מֹף וְנֹף בְּעָבְרְךָ בַּפֶּסַח. וַאֲמַרְתֶּם זֶבַח פֶּסַח.

יָ הּ רֹאשׁ כָּל אוֹן מָחַצְתָּ בְּלֵיל שִׁמּוּר פֶּסַח,
כַּ בִּיר עַל בֵּן בְּכוֹר פָּסַחְתָּ בְּדַם פֶּסַח,
לְ בִלְתִּי תֵּת מַשְׁחִית לָבֹא בִּפְתָחַי בַּפֶּסַח. וַאֲמַרְתֶּם זֶבַח פֶּסַח.

מְ סֻגֶּרֶת סֻגָּרָה בְּעִתּוֹתֵי פֶּסַח,
נִ שְׁמְדָה מִדְיָן בִּצְלִיל שְׂעוֹרֵי עֹמֶר פֶּסַח,
שֹׂ רְפוּ מִשְׁמַנֵּי פּוּל וְלוּד בִּיקַד יְקוֹד פֶּסַח. וַאֲמַרְתֶּם זֶבַח פֶּסַח.

ע וֹד הַיּוֹם בְּנֹב לַעֲמוֹד עַד גָּעָה עוֹנַת פֶּסַח,
פַּ ס יַד כָּתְבָה לְקַעֲקֵעַ צוּל בַּפֶּסַח,
צָ פֹה הַצָּפִית עָרוֹךְ הַשֻּׁלְחָן בַּפֶּסַח. וַאֲמַרְתֶּם זֶבַח פֶּסַח.

קָ הָל כִּנְּסָה הֲדַסָּה צוֹם לְשַׁלֵּשׁ בַּפֶּסַח,
רֹ אשׁ מִבֵּית רָשָׁע מָחַצְתָּ בְּעֵץ חֲמִשִּׁים בַּפֶּסַח,
שְׁ תֵּי אֵלֶּה רֶגַע תָּבִיא לְעוּצִית בַּפֶּסַח,
תָּ עֹז יָדְךָ תָּרוּם יְמִינְךָ כְּלֵיל הִתְקַדֵּשׁ חַג פֶּסַח. וַאֲמַרְתֶּם זֶבַח פֶּסַח.

TO HIM PRAISE IS PROPER, TO HIM PRAISE IS BECOMING

He is mighty in His dominions, truly supreme; His troops (of angels) say to Him: "To Thee alone, to Thee indeed, surely only to Thee; to Thee, O Lord, belongs the kingship.
To him praise is proper, to Him praise is becoming.

He is exalted in his dominions, truly honored; His faithful say to Him: "To Thee alone, to Thee indeed, surely only to Thee; to Thee, O Lord, belongs the kingship."
To Him praise is proper, to Him praise is becoming.

He is just in His dominions, truly powerful; His angels say to Him: "To Thee alone, to Thee indeed, surely only to Thee; O Lord, belongs the kingship."
To Him praise is proper, to Him praise is becoming.

He is the sole ruler in His dominion, truly all-powerful; His disciples (prophets) say to him: "To Thee alone, to Thee indeed, surely only to Thee; to Thee, O Lord, belongs the kingship."
To Him praise is proper, to Him praise is becoming.

He is the ruler in His dominion, truly awe-inspiring; His surrounding angels say to Him: "To Thee alone, to Thee indeed, surely only to Thee; to Thee, O Lord, belongs the kingship."
To Him praise is proper, to Him praise is becoming.

He is modest in His dominion, a true deliverer; His righteous say to Him: "To Thee alone, to Thee indeed, surely only to Thee; to Thee, O Lord, belongs the kingship."
To Him praise is proper, to Him praise is becoming.

He is holy in His dominion, truly merciful; His ministering angels say to Him: "To Thee alone, to Thee indeed, surely only to Thee; to Thee, O Lord, belongs the kingship."
To Him praise is proper, to Him praise is becoming.

He is mighty in His dominion, a true support; His perfect say to Him: "To Thee alone, to Thee indeed, surely only to Thee; to Thee, O Lord, belongs the kingship."
To Him praise is proper, to Him praise is becoming.

כִּי לוֹ נָאֶה. כִּי לוֹ יָאֶה:

אַדִּיר בִּמְלוּכָה, בָּחוּר כַּהֲלָכָה, גְּדוּדָיו יֹאמְרוּ לוֹ:
לְךָ וּלְךָ, לְךָ כִּי לְךָ, לְךָ אַף לְךָ, לְךָ יְיָ הַמַּמְלָכָה.
כִּי לוֹ נָאֶה, כִּי לוֹ יָאֶה.

דָּגוּל בִּמְלוּכָה, הָדוּר כַּהֲלָכָה, וָתִיקָיו יֹאמְרוּ לוֹ:
לְךָ וּלְךָ, לְךָ כִּי לְךָ, לְךָ אַף לְךָ, לְךָ יְיָ הַמַּמְלָכָה.
כִּי לוֹ נָאֶה, כִּי לוֹ יָאֶה.

זַכַּאי בִּמְלוּכָה, חָסִין כַּהֲלָכָה, טַפְסְרָיו יֹאמְרוּ לוֹ:
לְךָ וּלְךָ, לְךָ כִּי לְךָ, לְךָ אַף לְךָ, לְךָ יְיָ הַמַּמְלָכָה.
כִּי לוֹ נָאֶה, כִּי לוֹ יָאֶה.

יָחִיד בִּמְלוּכָה, כַּבִּיר כַּהֲלָכָה, לִמּוּדָיו יֹאמְרוּ לוֹ:
לְךָ וּלְךָ, לְךָ כִּי לְךָ, לְךָ אַף לְךָ, לְךָ יְיָ הַמַּמְלָכָה.
כִּי לוֹ נָאֶה, כִּי לוֹ יָאֶה.

מוֹשֵׁל בִּמְלוּכָה, נוֹרָא כַּהֲלָכָה, סְבִיבָיו יֹאמְרוּ לוֹ:
לְךָ וּלְךָ, לְךָ כִּי לְךָ, לְךָ אַף לְךָ, לְךָ יְיָ הַמַּמְלָכָה.
כִּי לוֹ נָאֶה, כִּי לוֹ יָאֶה.

עָנָו בִּמְלוּכָה, פּוֹדֶה כַּהֲלָכָה, צַדִּיקָיו יֹאמְרוּ לוֹ:
לְךָ וּלְךָ, לְךָ כִּי לְךָ, לְךָ אַף לְךָ, לְךָ יְיָ הַמַּמְלָכָה.
כִּי לוֹ נָאֶה, כִּי לוֹ יָאֶה.

קָדוֹשׁ בִּמְלוּכָה, רַחוּם כַּהֲלָכָה, שִׁנְאַנָּיו יֹאמְרוּ לוֹ:
לְךָ וּלְךָ, לְךָ כִּי לְךָ, לְךָ אַף לְךָ, לְךָ יְיָ הַמַּמְלָכָה.
כִּי לוֹ נָאֶה, כִּי לוֹ יָאֶה.

תַּקִּיף בִּמְלוּכָה, תּוֹמֵךְ כַּהֲלָכָה, תְּמִימָיו יֹאמְרוּ לוֹ:
לְךָ וּלְךָ, לְךָ כִּי לְךָ, לְךָ אַף לְךָ, לְךָ יְיָ הַמַּמְלָכָה.
כִּי לוֹ נָאֶה, כִּי לוֹ יָאֶה.

HE IS MIGHTY

He is mighty; soon will He rebuild His Temple; speedily, speedily, in our days. O God, rebuild, O God, rebuild; soon rebuild Thy Temple.

He is supreme, great and exalted; soon will He rebuild His Temple; speedily, speedily, soon in our days. O God, rebuild, O God, rebuild; soon rebuild Thy Temple.

He is honored, distinguished and just; soon will He rebuild His Temple; speedily, speedily, soon in our days; O God, rebuild, O God, rebuild; soon rebuild Thy Temple.

He is kind, pure and sole ruler; soon will He rebuild His Temple; speedily, speedily, soon in our days. O God, rebuild, O God, rebuild; soon rebuild Thy Temple.

He is all-powerful, omniscient and all-ruling; soon will He rebuild His Temple; speedily, speedily, soon in our days. O God, rebuild, O God, rebuild; soon rebuild Thy Temple.

He is glorious, great and powerful; soon will He rebuild His Temple; speedily, speedily, soon in our days. O God, rebuild, O God, rebuild; soon rebuild Thy Temple.

He is a redeemer, all-righteous, and most holy; soon will He rebuild His Temple; speedily, speedily, soon in our days. O God, rebuild; O God, rebuild; soon rebuild Thy Temple.

He is merciful, almighty and powerful; soon will He rebuild His Temple; speedily, speedily, soon in our days. O God, rebuild, O God, rebuild; soon rebuild Thy Temple.

אַדִּיר הוּא, יִבְנֶה בֵיתוֹ בְּקָרוֹב,
בִּמְהֵרָה בִּמְהֵרָה בְּיָמֵינוּ בְּקָרוֹב,
אֵל בְּנֵה, אֵל בְּנֵה, בְּנֵה בֵיתְךָ בְּקָרוֹב.

בָּחוּר הוּא, גָּדוֹל הוּא, דָּגוּל הוּא, יִבְנֶה בֵיתוֹ בְּקָרוֹב,
בִּמְהֵרָה בִּמְהֵרָה בְּיָמֵינוּ בְּקָרוֹב,
אֵל בְּנֵה, אֵל בְּנֵה, בְּנֵה בֵיתְךָ בְּקָרוֹב.

הָדוּר הוּא, וָתִיק הוּא, זַכַּאי הוּא, יִבְנֶה בֵיתוֹ בְּקָרוֹב,
בִּמְהֵרָה בִּמְהֵרָה בְּיָמֵינוּ בְּקָרוֹב,
אֵל בְּנֵה, אֵל בְּנֵה, בְּנֵה בֵיתְךָ בְּקָרוֹב.

חָסִיד הוּא, טָהוֹר הוּא, יָחִיד הוּא, יִבְנֶה בֵיתוֹ בְּקָרוֹב,
בִּמְהֵרָה בִּמְהֵרָה בְּיָמֵינוּ בְּקָרוֹב,
אֵל בְּנֵה, אֵל בְּנֵה, בְּנֵה בֵיתְךָ בְּקָרוֹב.

כַּבִּיר הוּא, לָמוּד הוּא, מֶלֶךְ הוּא, יִבְנֶה בֵיתוֹ בְּקָרוֹב,
בִּמְהֵרָה בִּמְהֵרָה בְּיָמֵינוּ בְּקָרוֹב,
אֵל בְּנֵה, אֵל בְּנֵה, בְּנֵה בֵיתְךָ בְּקָרוֹב.

נוֹרָא הוּא, סַגִּיב הוּא, עִזּוּז הוּא, יִבְנֶה בֵיתוֹ בְּקָרוֹב,
בִּמְהֵרָה בִּמְהֵרָה בְּיָמֵינוּ בְּקָרוֹב,
אֵל בְּנֵה, אֵל בְּנֵה, בְּנֵה בֵיתְךָ בְּקָרוֹב.

פּוֹדֶה הוּא, צַדִּיק הוּא, קָדוֹשׁ הוּא, יִבְנֶה בֵיתוֹ בְּקָרוֹב,
בִּמְהֵרָה בִּמְהֵרָה בְּיָמֵינוּ בְּקָרוֹב,
אֵל בְּנֵה, אֵל בְּנֵה, בְּנֵה בֵיתְךָ בְּקָרוֹב.

רַחוּם הוּא, שַׁדַּי הוּא, תַּקִּיף הוּא, יִבְנֶה בֵיתוֹ בְּקָרוֹב,
בִּמְהֵרָה בִּמְהֵרָה בְּיָמֵינוּ בְּקָרוֹב,
אֵל בְּנֵה, אֵל בְּנֵה, בְּנֵה בֵיתְךָ בְּקָרוֹב.

WHO KNOWS ONE?

Who know *one?* I know *one:* One is our God in heaven and on earth.

אֶחָד מִי יוֹדֵעַ, אֶחָד אֲנִי יוֹדֵעַ:
אֶחָד אֱלֹהֵינוּ שֶׁבַּשָּׁמַיִם וּבָאָרֶץ.

Who knows *two?* I know *two:* Two tablets of the covenant; one is our God in heaven and on earth.

שְׁנַיִם מִי יוֹדֵעַ, שְׁנַיִם אֲנִי יוֹדֵעַ:
שְׁנֵי לֻחוֹת הַבְּרִית,
אֶחָד אֱלֹהֵינוּ שֶׁבַּשָּׁמַיִם וּבָאָרֶץ.

Who knows *three?* I Know *three:* Three patriarchs; two tablets of the covenant, one is our God in heaven and on the earth.

שְׁלֹשָׁה מִי יוֹדֵעַ, שְׁלֹשָׁה אֲנִי יוֹדֵעַ:
שְׁלֹשָׁה אָבוֹת, שְׁנֵי לֻחוֹת הַבְּרִית,
אֶחָד אֱלֹהֵינוּ שֶׁבַּשָּׁמַיִם וּבָאָרֶץ.

Who knows *four?* I know *four:* Four mothers of Israel; three patriarchs; two tablets of the covenant; one is our God in heaven and on the earth.

אַרְבַּע מִי יוֹדֵעַ, אַרְבַּע אֲנִי יוֹדֵעַ:
אַרְבַּע אִמָּהוֹת, שְׁלֹשָׁה אָבוֹת, שְׁנֵי לֻחוֹת הַבְּרִית,
אֶחָד אֱלֹהֵינוּ שֶׁבַּשָּׁמַיִם וּבָאָרֶץ.

Who knows *five?* I know five: Five books of Moses; four mothers in Israel; three patriarchs; two tablets of the covenant; one is our God in heaven and on earth.

חֲמִשָּׁה מִי יוֹדֵעַ, חֲמִשָּׁה אֲנִי יוֹדֵעַ:
חֲמִשָּׁה חֻמְשֵׁי תוֹרָה, אַרְבַּע אִמָּהוֹת,
שְׁלֹשָׁה אָבוֹת, שְׁנֵי לֻחוֹת הַבְּרִית,
אֶחָד אֱלֹהֵינוּ שֶׁבַּשָּׁמַיִם וּבָאָרֶץ.

Who knows *six?* I know *six:* Six orders of the Mishnah; five books of Moses; four mothers in Israel; three patriarchs; two tablets of the covenant; one is our God in heaven and on earth.

שִׁשָּׁה מִי יוֹדֵעַ, שִׁשָּׁה אֲנִי יוֹדֵעַ:
שִׁשָּׁה סִדְרֵי מִשְׁנָה, חֲמִשָּׁה חֻמְשֵׁי תוֹרָה,
אַרְבַּע אִמָּהוֹת, שְׁלֹשָׁה אָבוֹת, שְׁנֵי לֻחוֹת הַבְּרִית,
אֶחָד אֱלֹהֵינוּ שֶׁבַּשָּׁמַיִם וּבָאָרֶץ.

Who knows *seven?* I know *seven:* Seven days in the week; six orders of the Mishnah; five books of Moses; four mothers of Israel; three patriarchs; two tablets of the covenant; one is our God in heaven and on earth.

שִׁבְעָה מִי יוֹדֵעַ, שִׁבְעָה אֲנִי יוֹדֵעַ:
שִׁבְעָה יְמֵי שַׁבַּתָּא, שִׁשָּׁה סִדְרֵי מִשְׁנָה,
חֲמִשָּׁה חֻמְשֵׁי תוֹרָה, אַרְבַּע אִמָּהוֹת,
שְׁלֹשָׁה אָבוֹת, שְׁנֵי לֻחוֹת הַבְּרִית,
אֶחָד אֱלֹהֵינוּ שֶׁבַּשָּׁמַיִם וּבָאָרֶץ.

Who knows *eight?* I know *eight:* Eight days of initiation; seven days in the week; six orders of the Mishnah; five books of Moses; four mothers of Israel; three patriarchs; two tablets of the covenant; one is our God in heaven and on earth.

שְׁמֹנָה מִי יוֹדֵעַ, שְׁמֹנָה אֲנִי יוֹדֵעַ:
שְׁמֹנָה יְמֵי מִילָה, שִׁבְעָה יְמֵי שַׁבַּתָּא,
שִׁשָּׁה סִדְרֵי מִשְׁנָה, חֲמִשָּׁה חֻמְשֵׁי תוֹרָה,
אַרְבַּע אִמָּהוֹת, שְׁלֹשָׁה אָבוֹת, שְׁנֵי לֻחוֹת הַבְּרִית,
אֶחָד אֱלֹהֵינוּ שֶׁבַּשָּׁמַיִם וּבָאָרֶץ.

Who knows *nine?* I know *nine:* Nine months of childbearing; eight days of initiation; seven days of the week; six orders of Mishnah, five books of Moses; four mothers of Israel; three patriarchs; two tablets of the covenant; one is our God in heaven and on earth.

תִּשְׁעָה מִי יוֹדֵעַ, תִּשְׁעָה אֲנִי יוֹדֵעַ:
תִּשְׁעָה יַרְחֵי לֵדָה, שְׁמֹנָה יְמֵי מִילָה,
שִׁבְעָה יְמֵי שַׁבַּתָּא, שִׁשָּׁה סִדְרֵי מִשְׁנָה,
חֲמִשָּׁה חֻמְשֵׁי תוֹרָה, אַרְבַּע אִמָּהוֹת,
שְׁלֹשָׁה אָבוֹת, שְׁנֵי לֻחוֹת הַבְּרִית,
אֶחָד אֱלֹהֵינוּ שֶׁבַּשָּׁמַיִם וּבָאָרֶץ.

Who knows *ten?* I know *ten:* Ten Commandments; nine months of childbearing; eight days of initiation; seven days of the week; six orders of the Mishnah; five books of Moses; four mothers of Israel; three patriarchs; two tablets of the covenant; one is our God in heaven and on earth.

עֲשָׂרָה מִי יוֹדֵעַ, עֲשָׂרָה אֲנִי יוֹדֵעַ:
עֲשָׂרָה דִבְּרַיָּא, תִּשְׁעָה יַרְחֵי לֵדָה,
שְׁמֹנָה יְמֵי מִילָה, שִׁבְעָה יְמֵי שַׁבַּתָּא,
שִׁשָּׁה סִדְרֵי מִשְׁנָה, חֲמִשָּׁה חֻמְשֵׁי תוֹרָה,
אַרְבַּע אִמָּהוֹת, שְׁלֹשָׁה אָבוֹת, שְׁנֵי לֻחוֹת הַבְּרִית,
אֶחָד אֱלֹהֵינוּ שֶׁבַּשָּׁמַיִם וּבָאָרֶץ.

Who knows *eleven?* I know *eleven:* Eleven stars (in Joseph's dream); ten commandments; nine months of childbearing; eight days of initiation; seven days of the week; six orders of Mishnah; five books of Moses; four mothers of Israel; three patriarchs; two tablets of the covenant; one is our God in heaven and on earth.

אַחַד עָשָׂר מִי יוֹדֵעַ, אַחַד עָשָׂר אֲנִי יוֹדֵעַ:
אַחַד עָשָׂר כּוֹכְבַיָּא, עֲשָׂרָה דִבְּרַיָּא,
תִּשְׁעָה יַרְחֵי לֵדָה, שְׁמֹנָה יְמֵי מִילָה,
שִׁבְעָה יְמֵי שַׁבַּתָּא, שִׁשָּׁה סִדְרֵי מִשְׁנָה,
חֲמִשָּׁה חֻמְשֵׁי תוֹרָה, אַרְבַּע אִמָּהוֹת,
שְׁלֹשָׁה אָבוֹת, שְׁנֵי לֻחוֹת הַבְּרִית,
אֶחָד אֱלֹהֵינוּ שֶׁבַּשָּׁמַיִם וּבָאָרֶץ.

Who knows *twelve?* I know *twelve:* Twelve tribes; eleven stars; ten commandments; nine months of childbearing; eight days of initiation; seven days of the week; six orders of the Mishnah; five books of Moses; four mothers of Israel; three patriarchs; two tablets of the covenant; one is our God in heaven and on earth.

שְׁנֵים עָשָׂר מִי יוֹדֵעַ, שְׁנֵים עָשָׂר אֲנִי יוֹדֵעַ:
שְׁנֵים עָשָׂר שִׁבְטַיָּא, אַחַד עָשָׂר כּוֹכְבַיָּא,
עֲשָׂרָה דִבְּרַיָּא, תִּשְׁעָה יַרְחֵי לֵדָה,
שְׁמֹנָה יְמֵי מִילָה, שִׁבְעָה יְמֵי שַׁבַּתָּא,
שִׁשָּׁה סִדְרֵי מִשְׁנָה, חֲמִשָּׁה חֻמְשֵׁי תוֹרָה,
אַרְבַּע אִמָּהוֹת, שְׁלֹשָׁה אָבוֹת, שְׁנֵי לֻחוֹת הַבְּרִית,
אֶחָד אֱלֹהֵינוּ שֶׁבַּשָּׁמַיִם וּבָאָרֶץ.

Who knows *thirteen?* I know *thirteen:* Thirteen attributes of God; twelve tribes; eleven stars; ten commandments; nine months of childbearing; eight days of initiation; seven days of the week; six orders of Mishnah; five books of Moses; four mothers of Israel; three patriarchs; two tablets of the covenant; one is our God in heaven and on earth.

שְׁלֹשָׁה עָשָׂר מִי יוֹדֵעַ, שְׁלֹשָׁה עָשָׂר אֲנִי יוֹדֵעַ:
שְׁלֹשָׁה עָשָׂר מִדַּיָּא, שְׁנֵים עָשָׂר שִׁבְטַיָּא,
אַחַד עָשָׂר כּוֹכְבַיָּא, עֲשָׂרָה דִבְּרַיָּא,
תִּשְׁעָה יַרְחֵי לֵדָה, שְׁמוֹנָה יְמֵי מִילָה,
שִׁבְעָה יְמֵי שַׁבַּתָּא, שִׁשָּׁה סִדְרֵי מִשְׁנָה,
חֲמִשָּׁה חֻמְשֵׁי תוֹרָה, אַרְבַּע אִמָּהוֹת,
שְׁלֹשָׁה אָבוֹת, שְׁנֵי לֻחוֹת הַבְּרִית,
אֶחָד אֱלֹהֵינוּ שֶׁבַּשָּׁמַיִם וּבָאָרֶץ.

AN ONLY KID

CHAD GADYA

Although the concluding song of the Seder service at first resembles a nursery rhyme, noted scholars point out that the song really is a history of successive empires that swallowed one another. The "one kid" is Israel; the cat is Assyria; the dog is Babylon; the stick is Persia; the water is Greece; the ox, Rome; the slaughterer, the Moslems; and the angel of death, the Crusaders. However, the Holy One will finally bring the reign of violence to an end and establish the Kingdom of the Almighty on earth. Perhaps a bear representing the Soviet Union should be included in modern day versions of Chad Gadya.

An only kid! An only kid, which my father bought for two zuzim (coins). An only kid!

חַד גַּדְיָא, חַד גַּדְיָא,
דִּזְבַן אַבָּא בִּתְרֵי זוּזֵי;
חַד גַּדְיָא, חַד גַּדְיָא.

Then came the cat and ate the kid, which my father bought for two zuzim. An only kid! An only kid!

וְאָתָא שׁוּנְרָא וְאָכַל לְגַדְיָא,
דִּזְבַן אַבָּא בִּתְרֵי זוּזֵי;
חַד גַּדְיָא, חַד גַּדְיָא.

Then came the dog and bit the cat, that ate the kid, which my father bought for two zuzim. An only kid! An only kid!

וְאָתָא כַלְבָּא וְנָשַׁךְ לְשׁוּנְרָא,
דְּאָכַל לְגַדְיָא, דִּזְבַן אַבָּא בִּתְרֵי זוּזֵי;
חַד גַּדְיָא, חַד גַּדְיָא.

Then came the stick and beat the dog, that bit the cat, that ate the kid, which my father bought for two zuzim. An only kid! An only kid!

וְאָתָא חוּטְרָא וְהִכָּה לְכַלְבָּא,
דְּנָשַׁךְ לְשׁוּנְרָא, דְּאָכַל לְגַדְיָא,
דִּזְבַן אַבָּא בִּתְרֵי זוּזֵי;
חַד גַּדְיָא, חַד גַּדְיָא.

Then came the fire and burned the stick, that beat the dog, that bit the cat, that ate the kid, which my father bought for two zuzim. An only kid! An only kid!

וְאָתָא נוּרָא וְשָׂרַף לְחוּטְרָא,
דְּהִכָּה לְכַלְבָּא, דְּנָשַׁךְ לְשׁוּנְרָא,
דְּאָכַל לְגַדְיָא, דִּזְבַן אַבָּא בִּתְרֵי זוּזֵי;
חַד גַּדְיָא, חַד גַּדְיָא.

Then came the water and quenched the fire, that burned the stick, that beat the dog, that bit the cat, that ate the kid, which my father bought for two zuzim. An only kid! An only kid!

וְאָתָא מַיָּא וְכָבָה לְנוּרָא,
דְּשָׂרַף לְחוּטְרָא, דְּהִכָּה לְכַלְבָּא,
דְּנָשַׁךְ לְשׁוּנְרָא, דְּאָכַל לְגַדְיָא,
דִּזְבַן אַבָּא בִּתְרֵי זוּזֵי;
חַד גַּדְיָא, חַד גַּדְיָא.

Then came the ox and drank the water, that quenched the fire, that burned the stick, that beat the dog, that bit the cat, that ate the kid, which my father bought for two zuzim. An only kid! An only kid!

וְאָתָא תוֹרָא וְשָׁתָה לְמַיָּא,
דְּכָבָה לְנוּרָא, דְּשָׂרַף לְחוּטְרָא,
דְּהִכָּה לְכַלְבָּא, דְּנָשַׁךְ לְשׁוּנְרָא,
דְּאָכַל לְגַדְיָא, דִּזְבַן אַבָּא בִּתְרֵי זוּזֵי;
חַד גַּדְיָא, חַד גַּדְיָא.

Then came the slaughterer and killed the ox, that quenched the fire, that burned the stick, that beat the dog, that bit the cat, that ate the kid, which my father bought for two zuzim. An only kid! An only kid!

וְאָתָא הַשּׁוֹחֵט וְשָׁחַט לְתוֹרָא,
דְּשָׁתָה לְמַיָּא, דְּכָבָה לְנוּרָא,
דְּשָׂרַף לְחוּטְרָא, דְּהִכָּה לְכַלְבָּא,
דְּנָשַׁךְ לְשׁוּנְרָא, דְּאָכַל לְגַדְיָא,
דִּזְבַן אַבָּא בִּתְרֵי זוּזֵי;
חַד גַּדְיָא, חַד גַּדְיָא.

Then came the angel of death and slew the slaughterer, that killed the ox, that drank the water, that quenched the fire, that burned the stick, that beat the dog, that bit the cat, that ate the kid, which my father bought for two zuzim. An only kid! An only kid!

וְאָתָא מַלְאַךְ הַמָּוֶת, וְשָׁחַט לַשּׁוֹחֵט,
דְּשָׁחַט לְתוֹרָא, דְּשָׁתָה לְמַיָּא,
דְּכָבָה לְנוּרָא, דְּשָׂרַף לְחוּטְרָא,
דְּהִכָּה לְכַלְבָּא, דְּנָשַׁךְ לְשׁוּנְרָא,
דְּאָכַל לְגַדְיָא, דְּזַבִּן אַבָּא בִּתְרֵי זוּזֵי;
חַד גַּדְיָא, חַד גַּדְיָא.

Then came the Holy One, blessed be He, and destroyed the angel of death, that slew the slaughterer, that killed the ox, that drank the water, that quenched the fire, that burned the stick, that beat the dog, that bit the cat, that ate the kid, which my father bought for two zuzim. An only kid! An only kid!

וְאָתָא הַקָּדוֹשׁ בָּרוּךְ הוּא, וְשָׁחַט לְמַלְאַךְ הַמָּוֶת,
דְּשָׁחַט לַשּׁוֹחֵט, דְּשָׁחַט לְתוֹרָא,
דְּשָׁתָה לְמַיָּא, דְּכָבָה לְנוּרָא,
דְּשָׂרַף לְחוּטְרָא, דְּהִכָּה לְכַלְבָּא,
דְּנָשַׁךְ לְשׁוּנְרָא, דְּאָכַל לְגַדְיָא,
דְּזַבִּן אַבָּא בִּתְרֵי זוּזֵי;
חַד גַּדְיָא, חַד גַּדְיָא.